what's your problem?

what's your problem?

To Solve Your Toughest Problems, Change the Problems You Solve

THOMAS WEDELL-WEDELLSBORG

HARVARD BUSINESS REVIEW PRESS
BOSTON, MASSACHUSETTS

Library of Congress Cataloging-in-Publication Data
Names: Wedell-Wedellsborg, Thomas, author.
Title: What's your problem? : to solve your toughest problems, change the problems you solve / Thomas Wedell-Wedellsborg.
Description: Boston : Harvard Business Review Press, [2020] | Includes index.
Identifiers: LCCN 2019041082 (print) | LCCN 2019041083 (ebook) | ISBN 9781633697225 (paperback) | ISBN 9781633697232 (ebook)
Subjects: LCSH: Problem solving. | Organizational effectiveness. | Reframing (Psychotherapy)
Classification: LCC HD30.29 .W434 2020 (print) | LCC HD30.29 (ebook) | DDC 658.4/03—dc23
LC record available at https://lccn.loc.gov/2019041082
LC ebook record available at https://lccn.loc.gov/2019041083

ISBN: 978-1-63369-722-5
eISBN: 978-1-63369-723-2

For Paddy Miller

contents

solve the right problem

what's your problem?

ARE YOU SOLVING THE RIGHT PROBLEMS?

We'll start with a question. Answer it for your team, your workplace, your society, your family, or just yourself:

How much do we waste—time, money, energy, even lives—by solving the wrong problems?

I have posed this question to people from all over the world, and rarely does anyone think the answer is insignificant. If your own reply gives you pause, consider a second question:

What if we could get better at solving the right problems?

What difference might it make to your life—to the people and the causes you care about—if everyone got just a little bit better at barking up the right trees?

This book is about how to do that. Its purpose is to upgrade the world's ability to solve problems. It does this by sharing a very specific skill called "reframing the problem," or "reframing" in short.

More than fifty years' of research has shown that reframing is an exceptionally powerful skill—and not just for solving problems. People who master reframing make better decisions, get more original ideas, and tend to lead more remarkable lives.

Best of all, it's not that hard to learn. By reading this book, you will become a better thinker and problem solver. You'll likely make headway on some of your current challenges, too—not later, but while you are reading this book.

To understand what reframing is, read on. A slow elevator is waiting for you.

THE SLOW ELEVATOR PROBLEM

Here's the central idea of this book:

The way you frame a problem determines which solutions you come up with.

By shifting the way you see the problem—that is, by reframing it—you can sometimes find radically better solutions.

To see how this works, consider this classic example, the slow elevator problem:

You are the owner of an office building, and your tenants are complaining about the elevator. It's old and slow, and they have to wait a lot. Several tenants are threatening to break their leases if you don't fix the problem.

First of all, notice how this problem isn't presented to you neutrally. Like most of the problems we encounter in the real world, someone has already framed it for you: *the problem is that the elevator is slow.*

In our eagerness to find a solution, many of us don't notice how the problem is framed; we take it for granted. As a result, we start coming up with ideas for how to make the elevator faster: Could we upgrade the motor? Could we improve the algorithm? Do we need to install a new elevator?

These ideas fall into a solution space, that is, a cluster of solutions that share assumptions about what the problem is:

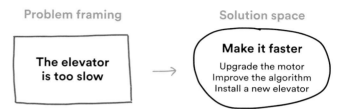

These solutions might work. However, if you pose this problem to building managers, they suggest a much more elegant solution: put up mirrors next to the elevator. This simple measure has proved effective in reducing complaints, because people tend to lose track of time when given something utterly fascinating to look at—namely themselves.

A BETTER PROBLEM TO SOLVE

The mirror solution doesn't solve the stated problem: it doesn't make the elevator faster. Instead it proposes a different understanding—that is, it reframes the problem:

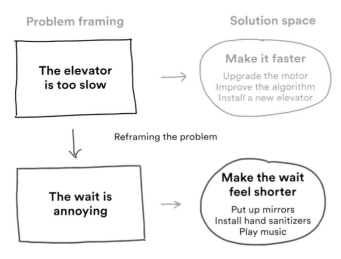

This is what reframing is about. At the heart of the method is a counterintuitive insight: sometimes, to solve a hard problem, *you have to stop looking for solutions to it.* Instead, you must turn your attention to the problem itself—not just to analyze it, but to shift the way you frame it.

A PROVEN, POWERFUL TOOL

The power of reframing has been known for decades, with people like Albert Einstein, Peter Drucker, and many others attesting to its importance. Combining innovation, problem solving, and asking the right questions, reframing is relevant no matter what you do, whether you're leading a team, launching a startup, closing a sale, crafting a strategy, dealing with a demanding customer, or doing any number of other things. It's useful for personal problems, too, as people work to build their careers, improve their marriages, or make their stubborn children marginally less stubborn. You can use reframing on pretty much any problem you face, in any area of your life, to resolve dilemmas and find new ways forward. Or as I like to put it: Everybody has problems. Reframing can help.

And help is needed—because most people haven't learned what reframing is, or how to do it. In fact, through my work, I have come to believe that reframing is the single biggest missing tool in our cognitive toolbox.

THE PROBLEM WITH PROBLEM SOLVING

Some years ago, a well-known *Fortune* 500 company hired me to teach reframing to 350 of its people. The session I taught was part of a week-long leadership program specially designed for the company's most talented leaders. To get into the room, you had to be in the top 2 percent of your peer group.

At the end of the week, we surveyed the participants and asked what they had found most useful. Among all the things people learned across five content-packed days, the two-hour session on reframing topped the list.

It was not the first time I had seen that reaction. Over the last decade, I've taught reframing to thousands of people from all over the world, and almost everyone says it is highly useful to them. Here are some typical reactions, taken verbatim from the feedback forms:

- "New way of looking at things is eye opening."

- "Loved it, absolutely opened my mind to a different way of thinking."

- "Reframe is a terrific concept that I had not been exposed to previously. I will directly use this as I work with my team in the future."

To me, these reactions were—and continue to be— deeply troubling.

Think about it: *Why on earth didn't these people know it already?* How come a group of really smart people working in a global *Fortune* 500 business—the top 2 percent of the company—doesn't already know how to solve the right problems?

In order to understand the extent of the problem, I surveyed 106 C-suite executives representing ninety-one private- and public-sector companies in seventeen countries. The result: **85 percent said that their organizations were not good at reframing.** Almost the same number said that their companies waste significant resources because of this.

This is a deep wrong. Reframing is a fundamental thinking skill. Frankly, this is stuff everyone should have been taught a long time ago. It is utterly crazy that we're not better at it. And it frightens me to consider how many mistakes are made every day because smart, talented people keep solving the wrong problems.

That is the problem this book aims to solve.

I've distilled my work over the last decade into a single, accessible guide to solving the right problems. The book's central framework is the **rapid reframing method**, a simple, proven approach you can use to tackle problems in almost any context. Crucially, the method is designed to be used *quickly*, as part of a busy everyday work environment: few of us can afford to take a slow approach to our problems.

I developed the method gradually over the last decade as I taught reframing to people of all stripes and seniority levels, helping them solve real-world problems. The strategies are based on prior research into problem solving and innovation. Beyond that, my selection of which strategies to include in the method wasn't based on any overarching theoretical model. I just chose the strategies that consistently proved most helpful to people in rethinking and solving their own problems—and that at the same time were broad enough to be useful across a wide range of problems and industries.

I have also validated the strategies through research in which I've studied how people solved thorny problems "in the wild," as an integral part of their day jobs rather than in a workshop setting. I have conducted numerous in-depth studies of how specific individuals went about solving hard problems and creating breakthrough innovations, working in everything from small startups to big, complex companies such as Cisco and Pfizer. While real-world reframing is certainly messier than a neat framework might suggest, each strategy represents approaches that have been used by practitioners to solve real-world problems and find new, creative ways to deliver results.

By reading this book you will:

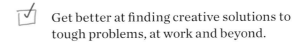 Get better at finding creative solutions to tough problems, at work and beyond.

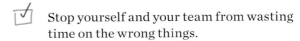 Stop yourself and your team from wasting time on the wrong things.

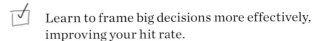 Learn to frame big decisions more effectively, improving your hit rate.

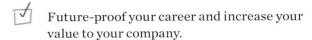 Future-proof your career and increase your value to your company.

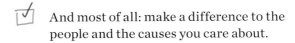 And most of all: make a difference to the people and the causes you care about.

Notably, the book is written for immediate application: as you move through it, chapter by chapter, you can start using the method right away to tackle your own problems. Here's how the book is laid out.

WHAT'S AHEAD

Part I: Intro — Reframing explained → **Part II: How to Reframe** — The method, step by step → **Part III: Overcome Resistance** — Complications and how to handle them

The coming chapter—**Reframing Explained**—quickly shares a few key concepts along with a remarkable real-world example of reframing.

Part II—**How to Reframe**—walks you through the reframing method step by step, with special emphasis on what questions to ask. Some things we'll cover:

- How a simple question—*what problem are we trying to solve*—stops people from falling in love with bad ideas

- Why expert practitioners *look outside the frame* before they dive into the details

- How *rethinking their goals* let a team reduce their workload by 80 percent

- How seeking and examining *positive exceptions* can lead to immediate breakthroughs

- Why *looking in the mirror* is key to solving interpersonal conflicts

- How two entrepreneurs used *problem validation* to spot a multimillion-dollar opportunity in two weeks

Already after reading part II, you will be fully equipped to use the method.

Part III—**Overcome Resistance**—is a resource you can consult as needed, offering suggestions for what to do when people resist the reframing process, when they won't listen to your advice, when they fall prey to silo thinking, and more.

Throughout the book, I'll also share lots of real-world examples of how reframing has led to big breakthroughs. These examples are mostly not about CEOs. Instead, most focus on what you might call "regular" people, in the best sense of the word *regular*. It's not that CEOs don't use reframing; several management scholars' research has shown that they do, to great effect. But serving as a CEO is a highly unusual job that has little in common with pretty much everyone else's daily work. My interest lies with how we improve problem solving not just in the boardroom but in every setting where we encounter problems. In short, I want to *democratize* reframing. The stories and the people you'll meet in this book reflect that focus.

You'll also be introduced to the most important research behind the concept. For more than half a century, reframing has been carefully studied by academics and practitioners from a wide range of fields—operations, psychology, math, entrepreneurship, design, philosophy, and many more—and this book owes a huge debt to their work. You'll meet some of the central reframing thinkers in the chapters ahead; many others are described in the endnotes. The book's website, www.howtoreframe.com, also offers a more in-depth research primer, useful if you want to understand the scientific evidence behind reframing (or if you just need some academic stardust to sprinkle over your client presentations).

THE REFRAMING CANVAS

Finally, I want to introduce the **reframing canvas**. The canvas provides an overview of the method's key steps, and you can use it with your team or clients to reframe problems. You can download free, printer-friendly versions on the book's website.

On the next page, you can see a high-level version of the canvas. Take a second to familiarize yourself with it, but don't worry about the details yet. We'll get there. For now, just notice that the method has three steps—Frame, Reframe, Move Forward—with some added strategies nested under the second step.

With that, let's get started.

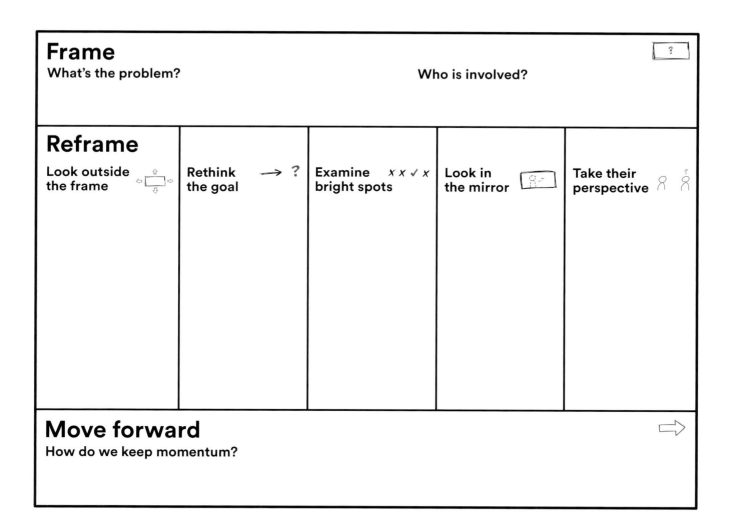

Frame

What's the problem?

Who is involved?

Reframe

Look outside the frame

Rethink the goal

Examine bright spots

Look in the mirror

Take their perspective

Move forward

How do we keep momentum?

reframing explained

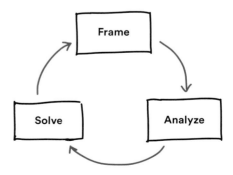

BEYOND ANALYSIS

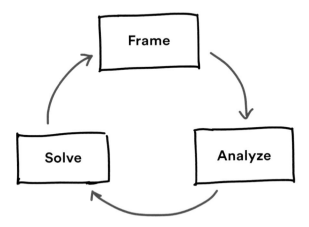

The most basic trait of good problem solvers is their optimism. When faced with a difficult situation, they don't just accept their fate. They believe that there is a better way forward—and that they are capable of finding it.

Optimism, though, is not enough. History is full of happy optimists running headfirst into walls. To succeed, their forward momentum must be coupled with the ability to take aim at the right problems. That is what reframing (and its first instance, framing) is about.

It's important to note that reframing is different from analyzing a problem. Analysis, as I use the term here, is when you ask, *Why is the elevator slow?* and try to understand the various factors that influence the speed. Being good at analysis is about being precise, methodical, detail-oriented, and good with numbers.

Reframing, in comparison, is a higher-level activity. It is when you ask, *Is the speed of the elevator the right thing to focus on?* Being good at reframing is not necessarily about the details. It is more about seeing the big picture and having the ability to consider situations from multiple perspectives.

Reframing is not limited to the start of the process, nor should it be done independent of the work of analyzing and solving the problem. On the contrary, your understanding of the problem will develop alongside your solution. As entrepreneurs and design thinkers alike will tell you, you can't hope to frame a problem correctly unless you get your hands dirty and test your thinking in the real world.

To show how this process works in practice, I'll share one of the most powerful examples I've found. It's a bit longer than the elevator story, but stick with me, there are puppies involved.

AMERICA'S SHELTER DOG PROBLEM

Americans love dogs: more than 40 percent of US households have one. But this fondness for the adorable four-legged fur dispensers has a downside: every year, it's estimated that more than three million dogs enter a shelter and are put up for adoption.

Shelters and other animal-welfare organizations work hard to raise awareness of this issue. A typical ad will show a neglected, sad-looking dog, carefully chosen to evoke compassion, along with a line such as "Save a life—adopt a dog" or perhaps a request for donations.

Through such initiatives, about 1.4 million dogs are adopted each year. But that leaves more than a million unadopted dogs, to say nothing of cats and other pets. Despite the impressive efforts of shelters and rescue groups, the shortage of pet adopters has persisted for decades.

There is some good news, though. Within the last few years, two small organizations have found new ways to address the issue. One of those is BarkBox, a New York–based startup that I have taught reframing to. BarkBox donates a percentage of its income to dogs in need, so one day, its nonprofit team decided to take a fresh look at the shelter dog problem.

Solve for access, not advertising

Given its small budget, BarkBox knew that investing in advertising wouldn't make much of a difference. Instead, it started looking for other ways to frame the problem. As Henrik Werdelin, cofounder of BarkBox and leader of the project, told me:

> We realized that the adoption issue was partially an *access* problem. Shelters rely heavily on the internet to showcase their dogs. However, their websites can be hard to find, and because the industry has so little money, the sites are rarely optimized for viewing on mobile devices. That was a problem I thought we could fix fairly easily.

The result, modeled on dating apps for humans, was a playful app called BarkBuddy, through which people could see profiles of adoptable dogs and contact the shelter that held them.

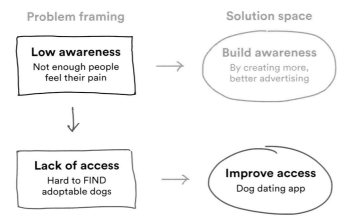

Launched with the tagline "Find fluffy singles in your area," the BarkBuddy app has since been downloaded more than 250,000 times. Soon after launch, it was serving up a million profile views every month. As the first dating app for dogs, BarkBuddy was also featured in several national TV programs and got airtime on a famous talk show. That is a fair amount of bark for your buck, if you will, given that the app cost about eight thousand dollars to build and launch.

This is classic reframing: by rethinking what the problem was, Werdelin and his team identified a new, more effective approach. But at the same time, you'll notice that in an important sense, the team was still working *within the original framing of the problem*: How do we get more dogs adopted? That's not the only way to frame the shelter problem.

A different approach: shelter intervention programs

Lori Weise is the executive director of Downtown Dog Rescue in Los Angeles and one of the pioneers behind the shelter intervention program. Lori's program doesn't seek to get more dogs adopted. Instead, it works to *keep the dogs with their first family* so they never enter the shelter system in the first place.

On average, about 30 percent of the dogs that enter a shelter are "owner surrenders," dogs deliberately relinquished by their owners. Within the volunteer-driven shelter community, united by its deep love of animals, such owners are often judged harshly: Exactly how heartless do you have to be to discard your dog like it was just some broken toy? To prevent dogs from ending up with such "bad" owners, many shelters—despite the chronic overpopulation of home-less dogs—require potential adopters to undergo laborious background checks, creating further barriers to adoption.

Lori saw things differently. As she told me, "The whole 'bad owner' story didn't sit well with me. I met many of these people in my work, and most of them care deeply about their dogs. They aren't bad people. That story was too simple."

To find out more, Lori set up a simple experiment at a shelter in South Los Angeles. Whenever a family came to hand over their dog, one of Lori's staff members would ask them, "If you could, would you prefer to keep your dog?"

If the family said yes, the staff member would then ask why the family was handing over their dog. If it was a problem that Lori and her staff could help fix, then they would, drawing on the group's funds and their industry connections.

Lori's experiment revealed a data point that flatly contradicted the industry's assumptions: 75 percent of owners said that they wanted to keep their dog. Many were in tears when handing over their dogs—and they had often taken good care of them for years before they came to the shelter. As Lori put it:

> "Owner surrenders" is not a people problem. By and large, it is a poverty problem. These families love their dogs as much as we do, but they are also exceptionally poor. We're talking about people who in some cases aren't entirely sure how they will feed their kids at the end of the month. So when a new landlord suddenly demands a deposit to house the dog, they simply don't have a way to get the money. In other cases, the dog needs a ten-dollar

rabies shot, only the family has no access to a vet, or may be wary of approaching any kind of authority. Handing over their pet to a shelter is often the last option they believe they have.

As Lori found, the intervention program wasn't just economically viable: it was actually more cost-effective than the group's other activities. Before the program, Lori's organization spent an average of around $85 per pet they helped. The new program brought that cost down to around $60 per pet, dramatically improving the organization's impact per dollar. The initiative also allowed the families to keep their beloved pets—and by keeping the pets out of the shelter, the program freed up space to help other animals in need.

Due to the work of Lori and several other pioneers, shelter intervention programs are being replicated across the United States, and the approach has gained the support of several industry organizations. As a consequence of this and other initiatives, the number of pets that end up in a shelter and the number that are euthanized are at all-time lows.

EXPLORING VERSUS BREAKING THE FRAME

The two stories illustrate the power of reframing. In both cases, by finding a new problem to solve, a small group of people managed to make a big difference. The stories also show how there are two different ways of reframing a problem—call it *exploring* versus *breaking* the frame.

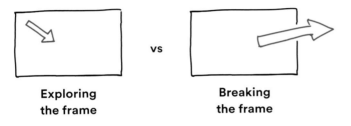

Exploring the frame | vs | Breaking the frame

Exploring the frame is when you delve deeper into the original problem statement.

It is similar to analyzing the problem, but with the added element that you keep an eye out for overlooked aspects of the situation that might make a difference. This is what the BarkBox team did. They started by saying "Not enough people adopt from shelters," and then they delved deeper until they spotted a "hidden" problem: the access issue. With the problem reframed, they created a wildly outsize impact from their eight thousand dollars' worth of investment.

Breaking the frame is when you step away completely from the initial framing of the problem.

Lori's program broke the frame. She rethought the very objective of her work—seeing it not as an adoption problem but as a problem of helping poor families keep their pets—and helped change her industry in the process.

Both of these approaches can lead to breakthroughs. But the idea of breaking the frame is more important, because if you don't master it, *you will get trapped by the initial framing of the problem*. Even for seasoned problem solvers, it's easy to get drawn into details, scouring a stated problem for clues while completely forgetting to challenge the overall framing. By keeping the idea of breaking the frame in mind, you will be less limited by how a problem happens to be framed when you first run into it.

TECHNICAL VERSUS MENTAL BREAKTHROUGHS

There is a second, more subtle difference between the two stories. The BarkBuddy story reads like a typical Silicon Valley tale: a hitherto overlooked problem was identified, and due to the amazing powers of technology, we now have a better way to solve it. The BarkBuddy app, in this sense, was deeply tied to its time. It wouldn't have been possible without smartphones, data-sharing standards, and a large population of people who had trained their thumbs on dating apps. Dartmouth professor Ron Adner calls this "the wide lens," meaning that for an innovation to succeed, a supporting ecosystem of technology and collaboration partners must already be in place.

Lori's invention had absolutely nothing to do with new technology, nor did it depend on having a large population previously trained in a new behavior. It certainly drew on a wide ecosystem of collaboration partners, including veterinarians and shelters—but all of those had been in place for decades, operating pretty much the same way.

This raises an interesting question: What was stopping us from coming up with the two solutions *earlier than we did*? BarkBuddy couldn't have been built much before it was. The conditions simply weren't in place. But Lori's shelter intervention program? Theoretically, we could have come up with that twenty or perhaps even forty years ago. The central barrier to its implementation wasn't technological. It was a wrongful belief—in this case, that the families who surrendered their dogs were all bad owners. For decades, an entire community had been blinded by its beliefs. Lori broke the frame by taking a piece of data everybody already knew and offering us a new way to understand it.

This is a key theme of the stories in this book. Innovators and problem solvers have an understandable fascination with new technology, whether it's engineers pushing the boundaries of physics, doctors developing new drugs, or programmers working wonders with bits and bytes.

But in a surprisingly large number of cases—especially those encountered in our daily lives—the solution to a problem depends not on technological but on mental breakthroughs. As such, solving tough problems is not always about the details, or about being a particularly systematic thinker. It can equally be about interpretation and sense-making; about seeing what is already there but rethinking what it means. Much depends on our ability to question our own beliefs, and to challenge assumptions that we may have held onto for a long time—about our colleagues, our customers, our friends and families, and not least ourselves.

––––––––––––

These stories have hopefully given you an idea of the difference reframing can make. To conclude this chapter, here are five specific benefits you'll gain from reading this book, explained in a bit more depth.

1. YOU WILL AVOID SOLVING THE WRONG PROBLEMS

Most people have a bias toward action. When faced with a problem, they immediately switch into solution mode, rejecting analysis in favor of rapid forward movement: *Why are we still talking about the problem? Let's find a solution, people!*

Action bias is generally a good thing: you don't want to get stuck in endless deliberation. But it carries the danger that people will charge ahead *without fully understanding the problem they are trying to solve*, or without considering whether they're taking aim at the right problem in the first place. As a consequence, they often waste their energy on the wrong things, fiddling with small variations on the same useless "solution" until they run out of time or money. Sometimes this is described as "rearranging the deck chairs on the *Titanic*."

The process I share in this book is designed to let you reframe problems fast, so you can get both the benefits of speed and the power of deliberation. By introducing reframing early in the process, before people fall in love with a specific solution, you can prevent wasted effort and achieve your goals faster.

2. YOU WILL FIND INNOVATIVE SOLUTIONS

Not everyone makes the mistake of jumping too quickly into action. Many have learned to spend time analyzing the problem. But even then they can miss important opportunities. Specifically, many people approach problem diagnosis by asking: *What is the real problem?* Guided by that question, they dig deep into the details, looking to find the "root cause" of the problem.

The elevator story highlights an important flaw in that way of thinking. The slowness of the elevator is presumably a real problem, and buying a new elevator would fix it. But crucially, *that is not the only way to see the problem*. In fact, the very idea that a single "root cause" exists can be misleading. Problems typically have multiple causes and can be addressed in many ways. The elevator problem could also be framed as a peak demand problem—too many people need the elevator at the same time—which could be solved by spreading out the demand, such as by staggering people's lunch breaks.

Reframing is not about finding the *real* problem; it's about finding a *better problem to solve*. By insisting that there is one correct interpretation of a problem, we blind ourselves to the possibility of smarter, more creative solutions. Reframing makes you better at finding those.

3. YOU WILL MAKE BETTER DECISIONS

Research has shown that one of the most powerful things you can do when solving problems is to **generate multiple options to choose from**. The Ohio State University professor Paul C. Nutt, a leading scholar in the field, found that people make bad decisions more than half the time when they consider only one real option:

- *Should I do an MBA or not?*

- *Should we invest in this project or not?*

In contrast, people who create and consider multiple options make the wrong call only a third of the time—and this holds true even if they end up sticking with their original plan in the end.

- *Shall I pursue an MBA, do a startup, seek a new job, or stay in my current role?*

- *Shall we invest in project A, B, or C, or is it better to hold off for now?*

Just increasing the options helps you make better judgment calls.

But there is a catch: the options you consider have to be *genuinely different*. A team that doesn't understand reframing may think their analysis was really thorough because they identified fifteen providers of new, faster elevators. Of course, they've just found fifteen different versions of the same solution. Reframing leads to better decisions because it lets you find genuinely different options to choose from.

And there's more. At the risk of doing what every author does with their favorite subject—*"and that, dear reader, is why furniture reupholstery will save humanity"*—I will nonetheless argue that the widespread mastery of reframing can have an even bigger positive impact. Take just two examples—one personal, one societal.

4. YOU WILL BROADEN YOUR CAREER OPTIONS

On a personal level, solving hard problems is one of the most fulfilling things there is, and it's a great way to make a difference for the people and causes you care about. On top of that, teaching yourself to reframe will also have some tangible effects on your career.

Most evidently, by becoming a better problem solver, you will immediately make yourself more valuable to your company. And because reframing doesn't require you to be a subject-matter expert for a given problem—as you'll see later, experts can sometimes get trapped by their own expertise—it also means that you can contribute to areas outside your own role, much like management consultants can add value to industries they haven't worked in themselves. That can be helpful in case you someday want to change into a different kind of role.

Not coincidentally, the ability to solve problems is also highly prized on the job market. In a recent report, the World Economic Forum shared a list of the most important skills for the future. The top three skills, listed here, should seem familiar:

1. Complex problem solving

2. Critical thinking

3. Creativity

Lastly, reframing will also future-proof your career in a very specific way: by making you less vulnerable to being replaced by a computer.

Depending on your current occupation, this threat may feel remote to you. However, most experts will give you a sobering message: AI and other forms of automation have already started taking over many of the jobs that people used to have, including white-collar jobs.

Problem diagnosis, though, is different. By its very nature, defining and reframing a problem is a uniquely human task, requiring a multifaceted understanding of the situation; an aptitude for absorbing vague, hard-to-quantify information; and the ability to interpret and rethink what the data means. These are all things that computers will not be capable of doing in the near-term future*—and as such, becoming better at them will serve to create both job security and new job opportunities for you.

5. YOU WILL HELP CREATE A HEALTHIER SOCIETY

Finally, reframing also matters to the continued functioning of our society. Solving conflicts in a sustainable way requires people to find common ground with their adversaries—and that often starts by figuring out what problems people are trying to solve, rather than fighting over solutions. As I'll show, reframing has been used to find new solutions to deeply entrenched political conflicts.

At the same time, learning to reframe is also a useful mental defense system—because research has shown that framing can be weaponized. Take a careful look at how people from warring political parties talk about a hot topic, and you will see how they use reframing to try to influence your thinking.

In this sense, reframing can be seen as a central civic skill. By boosting your problem-framing literacy, you will become better at detecting when someone is trying to manipulate you. A population more fluent in framing is a population better protected against demagogues and other people with ill intentions.

And that, dear reader, is why you should recommend this book to your allies, while softly slandering it to your political opponents.

---

*Well, no earlier than next Wednesday, anyway.

reframing explained

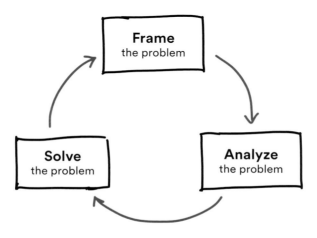

Tackling problems involves three activities that you cycle through repeatedly:

1. **Framing (and subsequently reframing) the problem:** when you determine what to focus on

2. **Analyzing the problem:** when you study the chosen framing of the problem in depth, trying to quantify it and understand the finer details

3. **Solving the problem:** the actual steps you take to fix it; things like experimentation, prototyping, and eventually implementing the full solution

There are two different ways to look for new angles on a problem:

1. **Exploring the frame:** when you try to reframe a problem by delving deeper into the details of the first framing

2. **Breaking the frame:** when you step away from the first framing, putting an entirely different spin on it

Most problems have multiple causes—and thus, they may have multiple viable solutions. People who look for the "real" problem risk missing out on creative solutions, because they stop at the first viable answer they find.

Not all solutions to problems are technical. Sometimes, new approaches can be found by questioning our beliefs rather than applying new technology.

Creating multiple options improves the quality of your decisions—provided those options are genuinely different.

Your career can benefit from reframing, as can our society as a whole.

part two

how to reframe

getting ready to reframe

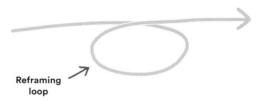

Reframing
loop

THE PROCESS

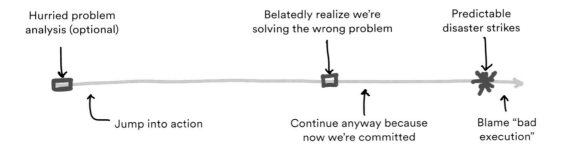

Hurried problem analysis (optional) → Jump into action

Belatedly realize we're solving the wrong problem → Continue anyway because now we're committed

Predictable disaster strikes → Blame "bad execution"

Most people recognize the danger, illustrated above, of jumping into action too rapidly. But what, exactly, is the alternative, given how busy everyone is? Sure, a leisurely latte-sipping author like me might have lots of time to engage in what a friend's daughter calls "thinky thoughts" (it's a technical term). People with real jobs generally don't have that luxury. When pressed for time, most of us opt to charge ahead, hoping that we'll be capable of cleaning up any resulting messes later.

That can create a vicious cycle. By not taking the time to ask questions, we create more problems for ourselves down the road, which in turn makes time even more scarce. As one senior executive described it: "We don't have time to invent the wheel, because we're so busy carrying around heavy stuff."

To get out of that trap, you first have to confront two flawed assumptions about problem diagnosis:

- It's a prolonged, time-intensive deep dive into the problem.

- You must complete this deep dive and understand the problem perfectly before taking any action.

These myths are captured in what is perhaps the world's most famous quotation on problem solving, often attributed to Albert Einstein: "If I had an hour to solve a problem and my life depended on it, I would spend fifty-five minutes defining the problem and then five minutes solving it."

It's a snappy quotation, for sure, but it's got some problems. For one, it's not actually from Einstein. The famed physicist was a strong believer in problem diagnosis, but there's no evidence that the "fifty-five minutes" quotation is from him. More important, even if Einstein had said it, it *still* would be poor advice. (As it happens, lessons from advanced theoretical physics don't necessarily transfer to everyday problem solving.) Here's what tends to happen if you manage your time according to the "Einstein" quotation:

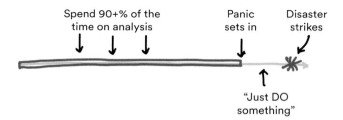

The common term for this is paralysis by analysis, and it often ends badly.

A BETTER APPROACH

Here's a better way to think about problem framing. First, think of problem solving as a straight line, indicating people's natural drive toward finding a solution:

Reframing is a loop off this path: a brief, deliberate redirection that temporarily shifts people's focus to the higher-level question of how the problem is framed. It results in getting back on the path with a new or improved understanding of the problem. If you like, think of it as a short break in the forward movement, like taking a step back from the action.

This reframing loop is repeated throughout the problem-solving journey, with multiple breaks during your forward movement. A team might start with a round of reframing on Monday, then switch into action mode for a week, and then revisit the problem on Friday, asking, *Did we learn something new about the problem, given what we did this week? Is our framing still correct?*

As you'll recall from the overview I shared earlier (the reframing canvas), the method has three steps—Frame, Reframe, Move Forward—with some nested strategies under the second step. In the following figure, you can see how this maps onto the loop.

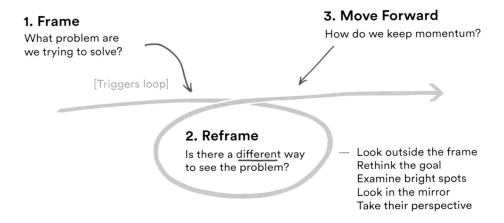

1. Frame
What problem are
we trying to solve?

3. Move Forward
How do we keep momentum?

[Triggers loop]

2. Reframe
Is there a <u>different</u> way
to see the problem?

— Look outside the frame
Rethink the goal
Examine bright spots
Look in the mirror
Take their perspective

Step 1—Frame

This is the trigger for the process. In practice, it starts with someone asking "What's the problem we're trying to solve?" The resulting statement—ideally written down—is your first framing of the problem.

Step 2—Reframe

Reframe is where you challenge your initial understanding of the problem. The aim is to rapidly uncover as many potential alternative framings as possible. You can think of it as a kind of brainstorming, only instead of ideas, you are looking for different ways to frame the problem. This might come in the form of

questions (*Why exactly is it a problem for people that the elevator is slow?*) or in the form of direct suggestions (*This might be a ploy to lower the rent*).

The five nested strategies can help you find these alternative framings of the problem. Depending on the situation, you may explore some, all, or none of these:

- **Look outside the frame.** *What are we missing?*

- **Rethink the goal.** *Is there a better objective to pursue?*

- **Examine bright spots.** *Where is the problem not?*

- **Look in the mirror.** *What is my/our role in creating this problem?*

- **Take their perspective.** *What is their problem?*

Step 3—Move Forward

This closes the loop and switches you back into action mode. This can be a continuation of your current course, a move to explore some of the new framings you came up with, or both.

Your key task here is to determine how you can *validate the framing of your problem* through real-world testing, making sure your diagnosis is correct. (Think of a doctor who makes a diagnosis—*this looks a lot like meningitis*—and then orders a test to confirm her diagnosis before starting the treatment.) At this point, a subsequent reframing check-in may be scheduled as well.

WHAT TOOLS DO I NEED FOR REFRAMING?

You don't need any materials in order to reframe a problem, but **flip charts or whiteboards** are helpful, especially with groups. Shared writing surfaces keep people engaged and collaborating.

Checklists can help too. In the back of this book, you'll find a checklist you can put up in your workspace.

For really important problems—or for when you need to create legitimacy around the process—use the **reframing canvas**. You'll find extra copies of the canvas in the back of this book, and can download free printer-friendly versions as well on the book's website.

WHO SHOULD BE INVOLVED?

You can reframe a problem on your own—and sometimes that's a good way to start, just to get your own thoughts in order. But usually you should *get other people involved as quickly as possible*. Sharing your problem with others—especially people who are different from you—provides an extremely powerful shortcut to new perspectives and can help you detect blind spots in your thinking much more rapidly.

If you start small, I recommend working in groups of three rather than two. A three-person group allows one person to listen and observe while the other two talk.

For better effect, involve outsiders in the process—people who are not as close to the problem as you and your immediate connections. Involving outsiders takes more effort, but with important problems in particular, it tends to be worth it.

Beyond that, there are no particular limits or requirements around group size. It's more a matter of what's practically possible. If it's feasible to share your problem widely, such as on a corporate intranet or even on social media, go ahead and try it.

WHEN SHOULD I USE THE PROCESS?

As often as needed. Don't assume that a problem has to be a certain size for reframing to work. Instead, modify the reframing process to fit the size of the problem.

At one end of the reframing spectrum, there's what you might call **improvised reframing**. Say, a colleague ambushes you in the hallway asking for help, or a problem suddenly comes up during a phone call with a client. In such situations, being methodical is rarely viable. Instead, just ask what the problem is, and then use your intuition to zoom in on the one or two angles that seem most promising for reframing.

At the other end of the spectrum is **structured reframing**, situations in which you can apply the process methodically. It could be when you're running a meeting and can use the canvas, or when you are sitting down to think through one of your own problems, like you can do while reading this book.

Of the two, improvised reframing is the most important to master, because reframing is more *a way of thinking* than a process. The psychologist and education expert Stephen Kosslyn talks about "habits of mind," simple mental routines that, once learned, can be used on most problems you encounter. In time,

you'll get to a point where you can reframe problems on the fly, without having to rely on the presence of a checklist.

Using more structured versions, however, is still a fantastic way to gain practice with the method, either individually or as a group, and will help you get much better at doing it on the fly. As you read through this book, I recommend using either a checklist or the canvas to think through some of your own problems as well (more on that in a minute).

HOW LONG SHOULD IT TAKE?

Fully analyzing a problem can take time—but figuring out *whether it's the right problem to analyze* doesn't have to. Once you've gotten some practice, spending just five to fifteen minutes on the middle part (the actual reframing) often will be sufficient.

This may raise eyebrows with people who are new to reframing. Hearing it can go this quickly, they tend to reply, *Five minutes? That's not enough to even explain my problem, much less reframe it.*

Sure, some problems are indeed so complicated that more time is needed. But in other cases, you'll find that problems can successfully be reframed very rapidly, based on only the most superficial description of the issue. In my workshops, when I ask people to try the method on a personal problem for just five minutes, there's often one or two people who experience breakthroughs just from that first exercise—sometimes on a problem they've struggled with for months or longer.

Incidentally, I'm not the only one who's found that quick applications can work. The MIT professor Hal Gregersen, a fellow problem-solving scholar, advocates for an exercise called "question bursts," in which he gives people a total of two minutes to explain their problem, followed by four minutes of group questioning. As Gregersen puts it, "People often believe that their problems require detailed explanations, but quickly sharing the challenge forces you to frame it in a high-level way that doesn't constrain or direct the questioning."

Many problems will *not* yield a-ha! moments after just five minutes. Some require multiple rounds of reframing, interspersed with experimentation. But even when that's the case, the initial round of reframing is still crucial, as it can open the door to later insights, once the questions have had some time to settle in. I generally recommend multiple short rounds of reframing rather than prolonged sessions, simply because the ability to use reframing in short bursts is crucial to making it useful in an everyday setting. The longer you make the process, the less you'll use it.

DOES THE ORDER OF THE STRATEGIES MATTER?

With the strategies listed in step 2 (Reframe), you don't necessarily have to stick to the sequence. When solving problems as part of a quick workplace conversation, feel free to jump straight to the particular strategy that seems most promising given the problem at hand.

There's one partial exception to this, though, and that's "take their perspective," which is about understanding the stakeholders. When facing a problem, many people are tempted to jump straight into that: *Peter got upset, you say? Is anything going on with him?* In my framework, however, you'll notice that it's one of the last steps. This is deliberate. The big problem with starting with the stakeholder analysis is that you can get trapped in trying to take the perspective *of the wrong group of people.*

The innovation expert Clayton Christensen, among others, has observed that innovation often comes not from studying your customers but from studying people who aren't your customers. In fact, as Christensen pointed out in his work on disruptive innovation, when companies focus too hard on understanding and serving the needs of their existing customers, they inadvertently make their products less useful for noncustomers, creating an opening for competitors to move in. In sum: start by thinking about goals and bright spots, and by asking if there are any other stakeholders you should be paying attention to (look outside the frame). Dive into the stakeholders only once you are fairly sure you are looking at the right people.

———————

One more note: in this book, you'll find lots of sample questions you can use to reframe problems. But they are exactly that: samples. Unlike the Harry Potter series, there are no magic words you have to memorize and then intone in exactly the right sequence to succeed.

I highlight this because some problem-solving frameworks place great emphasis on using precisely worded phrases, such as the opener "how might we" or the oft-repeated advice to ask "why" five times. Standard phrases like these can be very helpful at times. But at the same time, when it comes to reframing, I have become cautious of relying too much on formulaic questions.

Real-world problems are generally way too diverse for one-size-fits-all questions to work. Even in situations when a specific question did turn out to be pivotal, we can place too great an emphasis on what the question was. The important thing, in my experience, is not the exact question but rather the underlying thinking that led someone to ask that question.

Standard questions also fail to take cultural norms of communication into account. Most obviously, this is true if you work internationally. Less obviously, this is also true for the more local contexts. Pitch meetings and parent-teacher meetings call for different forms of inquiry, as do courtrooms and carpools or, for that matter, boardrooms and bedrooms.

Even a question as basic as, *Are we solving the right problem?* will be better phrased in some contexts as *Are we focusing on the right things here?* I've worked with some organizations where people preferred to talk about "challenges" or "improvement opportunities" rather than "problems," in order to sound less negative. Personally, I lean toward calling a problem a problem—*Houston, we have an improvement opportunity*—but the context you are in may require a different tack.

Ultimately, questioning is important because it reflects a spirit of curiosity. People who ask questions understand that the world is deeper and more complex than their current mental models might suggest. They understand that they might be wrong, which is the first step to finding better answers. Adhere too rigidly to a standard way of asking questions, and you risk missing out on the power of that mindset.

For that reason, as you read this book, seek to understand the essence of each strategy: What is the intent of the questions that are asked? Focus on how to think, not on what to say.

getting ready to reframe

WHAT'S YOUR PROBLEM?

With most books, we first absorb the ideas and then put the ideas to use when we're done reading. With this book, you can use it on your own problems *while you read it*, applying the method chapter by chapter.

I wrote the book so you can do either, knowing that some people prefer just to get the ideas. But I recommend trying to apply the method as you go. You'll get better at reframing while gaining fresh perspectives on some of your problems.

If you take that path, here's some advice that will help you maximize your learning from the process.

How to select your problems

Normally, when using reframing, you'd simply pick whatever problem you care about the most. But here, you are also learning the method of reframing, so I suggest the following approach:

Pick two problems. Real-world problems are diverse. Not every strategy will be useful for—or even applicable to—a specific problem. By picking two problems, you will get to use and practice more of the strategies.

Pick problems from different areas. I suggest you select a *work-related problem* and a problem from your *personal life*.

Why a personal-life problem too? Isn't that a bit self-helpy? Will I shortly go all New Age on you, recommending herbal teas and chakra readings?

Not quite. I've found personal problems to be ideal "trainer" problems as you work to master the method. And of course, the two worlds are closely related: solving a problem at home often means you'll have more energy for challenges at work, and vice versa.

Pick problems that aren't too basic. Everybody has minor frictions in their lives: laundry, long commutes, email overload, and whatnot. Issues like these can certainly be reframed—but for the purposes of learning the method, they are rarely the most useful ones to work on, because they're too simple. (I remember one client, for example, who stated his problem as: "Rabbits are eating the fruits in my garden!" This was not a metaphor for anything, sadly, and unlike the rabbits in question, the ensuing attempts at reframing were less than fruitful.)

Instead, I suggest you pick *people-related problems.* Reframing is particularly potent when it comes to "fuzzy" problems such as leadership, peer relationships, parenting, or even just self-management (e.g., a bad habit you want to get rid of).

I also suggest picking *problems that you feel less comfortable with*, or that you might even hesitate to face. These might be:

- **Situations you don't handle well.** *I really struggle with networking. I have a hard time making my voice heard in client meetings. It stresses me out when I have to give people negative feedback.*

- **Difficult relationships.** *I find it draining to deal with client X. Conversations with my boss/colleague/oldest child go south way too often. I feel like I don't have a handle on my new role in this team.*

- **Managing yourself.** *Why on earth am I always so bad at being disciplined? What should I do to really live up to my potential? I really wish I could find a way to live out my more creative side.*

It's also a good idea to pick problems that you've tried to solve before. When problems have resisted multiple prior attempts to solve them, it's a sign that they could benefit from reframing.

For now, pick the problems you'd like to work on, and then make a note of each one. I would recommend writing them on either a separate piece of paper or a Post-it note, so you can revisit them later—or you can use the reframing canvas (tear out one from the back, or download and print it).

At the end of each chapter, I'll guide you in how to use the reframing techniques in that chapter on the problems you've chosen. And if you have trouble picking problems, I've provided some inspiration on the next page.

Relationships

Friends, lovers, landlords. Business partners, pesky neighbors, parking guards. In-laws. Take your pick.

Leadership

Making people follow you. Fostering passion. Developing talent. Blaming failure on others. The usual.

Productivity

Getting more time. Making the most of scarce resources. Improving output.

Purpose

Why am I here? What do I want to do with my life? How do I shape my career and find meaning, happiness, etc.?

Innovation

Making it happen in your business, one way or the other. Creating the future. Avoiding obsolescence.

What's <u>Your</u> Problem?

Just in case you are one of those annoyingly issues-free people who need help remembering your problems

Bosses

Need I say more?

Growth

Where is it going to come from? How do we beat the competition?

Children

Like bosses, only worse. Our cute and demented masters.

The big picture

Ending hunger. Eradicating disease. Preserving democracy. Fixing broken systems. Saving our planet. Colonizing Mars. Harnessing artificial intelligence. Vanquishing aging, death, and self-assembly furniture.

Dating

Meeting Mr./Miss Right. Avoiding idiots. Not conflating the two. Failing at this. Starting over.

Money

Making more of it. Spending less of it. Or at least spending it on better things.

frame the problem

On the monitor of the designer Matt Perry's computer sits a yellow Post-it with a simple question:

What problem are we trying to solve?

Matt works at *Harvard Business Review*. Along with Scott Berinato, Jennifer Waring, Stephani Finks, Allison Peter, and Melinda Merino, he is part of the team that created this book. Right after our first meeting in their airy Boston offices, Matt emailed me:

I've had this one constant Post-it on my monitor for about a year now. It's a simple question, but such a helpful reminder on so many occasions. And that's why this particular note has stuck around (ha!)

on my monitor—unlike some others that aren't as timeless.

At first glance, the emphasis on simply stating the problem seems puzzling. Isn't it pretty obvious that you need to do that? Why did this particular Post-it get to stick around instead of some other piece of timeless designer wisdom? ("Always dress in black.")

Talk to anyone who solves other people's problems for a living—not just designers but lawyers, doctors, management consultants, coaches, or psychologists—and you will find the same strong insistence: start by asking what the problem is.

That's where the reframing process starts too. Simply put, you should:

- Create a short **problem statement**, ideally by writing down the problem as a full sentence: "The problem is that . . ." If you work with a group, use a flip chart so everyone looks at the same surface.

- Draw up a **stakeholder map** next to the statement that lists the people who are involved in the problem. Stakeholders can be both individuals and things like companies or business units.

Keep in mind:

Writing it down is important. Simple as it seems, putting a problem into writing brings a host of important benefits. Do it if at all possible.

Write it down **fast.** The problem statement isn't intended to be a perfect description of the issue. It's simply raw material for the process that follows. Think of it as a slab of wet clay that you plonk down on the table, giving you something tangible to dig into as you start working.

Use full sentences. Using bullet points or one-word problem descriptions makes it harder to reframe.

Keep it short. Reframing works best when you limit the problem description to a few sentences.

If you decided to work on some of your own challenges, I suggest you pause here and create problem statements and stakeholder maps for each problem before continuing. Use a separate piece of paper for each problem.

WHY WRITE DOWN YOUR PROBLEMS?

There are many benefits to writing down your problem. Here are some of them:

- **It slows things down a bit.** Writing creates a brief, natural thinking space that redirects the momentum and prevents people from jumping prematurely into solution mode.

- **It forces you to be specific.** Problems can be strangely fuzzy when they exist inside your head. Putting them in writing creates clarity.

- **It creates mental distance.** It's easier to look objectively at a problem once it exists as a physical thing separate from yourself.

- **It gives advisers more to work with.** It's easier for advisers to help you when they have a written problem statement in front of them. Writing dramatically expands the number of items people can keep in their mental workspace.

- **It creates an anchor for the discussion.** When people come up with ideas, you can quickly point to the statement and ask, *Does that idea solve this* *problem?* (Sometimes, an idea might make you change the problem statement; that's fine too. The point isn't to stick to your first framing but to keep both perspectives—problems and solutions—in view.)

- **It creates a paper trail.** If you are working for a client, having a written problem statement can help you avoid conflicts down the road. People's memories are fallible, and without a problem statement, there is a risk that clients will start misremembering what problem they asked you to solve.

WHAT'S YOUR PROBLEM TYPE?

Once you have a problem statement in front of you, the next step is to review it. To prepare for the review, we'll take a quick detour to the early days of problem-framing research in order to explore some of the different ways problems present themselves.

––––––––––––

In the 1960s, about a decade after the field of creativity research was founded, the influential educator Jacob Getzels made a key observation. He noted that the problems we're trained on in school are often quite different from the ones we encounter in real life.

In school, problems tend to present themselves in a nice, orderly manner: *Here's a triangle! If one side is blah blah blah, what is the length of the third side?* Con-

veniently, the problem appears at the end of a chapter on Pythagoras' theorem, giving us a pretty good idea about how we might solve it. Getzels called these *presented problems*, ones in which our job is to implement a solution without screwing up too badly along the way.

In the first jobs we get, presented problems are common: *The boss needs an overview of the latest market data. Review these three reports and prepare a summary for her.* But as we progress in our careers and start dealing with more-complex matters, problems increasingly appear in three other forms, each of which presents special challenges:

1. An ill-defined mess or pain point

2. A goal we don't know how to reach

3. A solution someone fell in love with

To master the art of problem diagnosis—Getzels talked about the idea of *problem finding*—it's helpful to understand the three types in more depth.

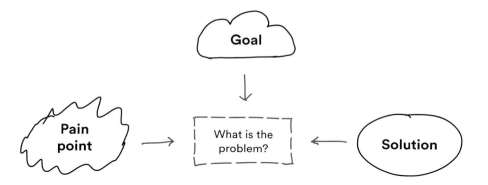

Problem type 1: an ill-defined mess or pain point

Before we formally recognize problems, we feel them, as ill-defined "issues" or pain points. Some are sudden, dramatic, and acutely felt: *Our sales are dropping like a rock*. Others are more subtle and slow-burning, carrying a sense of quiet desperation: *My career feels like it has stalled. Our industry is in decline. My sister is on a bad path.*

Often, the cause of the pain is unclear. Within clinical psychology, for instance, the psychotherapist Steve de Shazer estimated that when starting therapy, two out of three patients initially couldn't point to a specific problem they wanted to solve. The phenomenon occurs with workplace problems too. For example, when people say "Our culture is the problem," it can reliably be interpreted as "We have no clue what the problem is."

Pain points often cause people to jump to solutions without pausing to consider what's going on. Here are some typical examples. Notice the effortless move from pain point to solution.

- Our new product isn't selling. *We need to invest more in marketing.*

- Surveys show that 74 percent of our staff often feels disengaged. *We've got to get better at communicating our corporate purpose.*

- There are too many safety violations in our factory. *We need clearer rules and maybe stronger penalties, too.*

- Our employees are resisting the reorganization efforts. *We need to roll out some training so they can learn to ~~do as they are told~~ embrace change.*

In some cases, the solutions people jump to are based on dubious logic. *My stressed-out spouse and I fight all the time. Having a baby or five would surely calm things down around here.* More often, though, the solution will seem quite rational, and may have proven effective in other circumstances—only, in this case, it isn't aimed at the problem you are actually facing.

Problem type 2: a goal we don't know how to reach

Problems can also present themselves in the shape of a hard-to-reach goal. A classic business example is the so-called growth gap: the leadership team has set a target of twenty million in revenue, but regular sales will get us only to seventeen million. How on earth do we generate another three million in revenue? Mission statements and new-CEO growth strategies are also frequent sources of such goals: *we want to become the market leader in X.*

When you are facing a pain point, you at least have some kind of starting point to explore. Goals don't necessarily have that: you may be entirely clueless in terms of where to start. *How do I find a long-term romantic partner? My current method of shouting at strangers in the street seems to have some deficiencies.*

All you know is that your current behavior won't suffice. Hard-to-reach goals require people to come up with new ideas rather than sticking to business as usual. (This, of course, is one reason leaders like to set them.)

In a problem-solving context, goal-driven problems are first and foremost characterized by a need for *opportunity identification.* While opportunity identification has mostly been studied by innovation scholars, not problem-solving researchers, the skills required to do it are nonetheless closely related to reframing and problem finding. For instance, many successful innovations hinge on rethinking what customers really care about, versus what the existing solutions in the market cater to.

Problem type 3: someone fell in love with a solution

The most challenging scenario is when you are presented with a demand for a solution. Imagine a graphic designer's client says, "I need a big green button on my website." A novice designer will simply create the button, after which there are pretty good odds the client will come back and complain, "The button didn't work!" (Or better yet, "When I said green button, you should have known that I really meant red switch.") If you don't understand the problem to be solved, giving people what they ask for can be a bad idea.

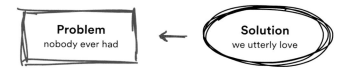

Once you start looking, you'll find that the solution-first dynamic is everywhere. Here are a few examples, one of which you'll encounter later in this book:

- "We should build an app!"

- "I'm dreaming of starting a business that sells Italian ice cream."

- "I saw this cool website where employees can share their ideas. We should get one of those."

Sometimes, people have fallen in love with an idea—we should do X!—with zero evidence that the solution they are dreaming of solves a real-world problem. (*What problem are we solving, you ask? Well, making a dent in the universe, evidently.*) This is sometimes called a solution in search of a problem. Those scenarios can be particularly problematic, because a bad solution can do more than just waste time and money. It can also do active harm.

In another popular variation, the solution is disguised as a problem. With the slow elevator example, for instance, your landlord may come to you and say, "We need to find money to pay for the new elevator. Can you help me figure out what to cut from the budget?"

REVIEW THE PROBLEM

Before applying any specific reframing strategies, it's a good practice to start with a general review of the problem statement.

Below, I have outlined some questions that can help you do that. The list will start to develop your problem literacy, meaning your general attunement to how problems are framed. The list also highlights typical instances of reframing that weren't big enough to merit their own chapters, but which are still important to keep an eye out for.

Here are the questions:

1. Is the statement true?

2. Are there simple self-imposed limitations?

3. Is a solution "baked into" the problem framing?

4. Is the problem clear?

5. With whom is the problem located?

6. Are there strong emotions?

7. Are there false trade-offs?

1. Is the statement true?

When I share the slow elevator problem, many people forget to ask a basic question about the framing: *Is the elevator actually slow?*

Somehow, because the tenants say it is slow, this is taken as a fact about the world. But of course, many other things could be going on: it could be a perception issue, an attempt to lower the rent, or something else.

When looking at a problem statement, a good first question to ask is, *How do we know this is true? Could this be incorrect?*

- *Are our shipments actually arriving late in this market? How is the tracking data created?*

- *How reliable is this report about weapons of mass destruction?*

- *Is our son's math teacher really as incompetent as I think? How did his prior students do in the final exams?*

- *Is it possible that the reports of my death have been greatly exaggerated?*

2. Are there simple self-imposed limitations?

Sometimes, merely by reading the problem description, you will realize that you have imposed an unnecessary constraint on the solution.

Take the experience of my brother, Gregers Wedell-Wedellsborg. Back in the early days of the mobile internet, Gregers was working at the Danish broadcaster TV2 when some of his employees came to him with an idea: *How about trying to develop content for viewing on mobile phones?*

Gregers liked the idea, but faced a problem: since mobile content was unknown territory at the time, there was no established model for making money on it—and TV2 was facing financial cutbacks at the time. For that reason, getting it onto that year's budget would be a hard sell. Maybe the following year it would be possible.

However, Gregers quickly realized that the problem had been too narrowly defined—because who said the money had to come from TV2's coffers? He really just needed a bit of cash to start the project. Could that be found elsewhere? He told his team to go outside TV2 to look for potential funding from partners.

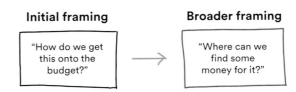

The team found the funding. Danish mobile operators were very interested in having TV2 develop mobile content, as the high-volume video content would increase their earnings from data traffic and boost sales of smartphones. The experiment went ahead and eventually launched TV2's venture into the mobile market, making it a market leader at almost no cost to TV2.

To find self-imposed limitations, simply review the framing of the problem and ask: *How are we framing this? Is it too narrow? Are we putting constraints on the solution that aren't necessarily real?*

3. Is a solution "baked into" the problem framing?

Some years ago, I cotaught an MBA elective in which we had the students do an innovation project. Here's how one of the teams described their project:

We want to develop better nutrition education to promote healthier eating at the school.

The statement contains a glaring assumption: namely that lack of knowledge prevents people from eating healthier food. That's a questionable problem framing. The vast majority of business-school students are aware of what is and isn't healthy. *French fries count as vegetables, right?* said nobody ever.

In a similar manner, people often frame problems in a way that points toward a specific solution. Consider this problem statement from a corporate initiative I was involved in that aimed at promoting gender equality.

Problem

We have not empowered enough female leaders to become effective and visible role models.

Notice that a solution—*let's create more female role models*—is baked into the initial problem statement. The point is not whether this particular diagnosis was correct. The important thing is to *notice* the framing, allowing you to question it.

People who don't do reframing might ask a follow-up question such as, *How do we help more women become role models?* and thereby get trapped, potentially, in an unhelpful or suboptimal framing.

In contrast, people who are trained in reframing will ask such questions as, *Are there other things in play? How about our promotion processes? How about informal connections? Do women get less exposure to senior decision makers?*

The mere act of asking those questions makes it more likely you'll pick a good solution, even if you stick with the first diagnosis in the end.

4. Is the problem clear?

In the previous example, the team had a fairly clear problem statement, which is a good starting point for the reframing process. In comparison, take a look at this one, also from a client:

> The problem is that we need to improve profitability of new client acquisition (top line revenue).

This statement is not actually a problem. It's a goal written as a problem, with a bit of added specificity about where they hope the revenue will come from. A "problem" statement like this typically means that the team has to shift their perspective from *their* problem to identifying a problem that *clients* care about—such as, what makes it attractive for new clients to sign up? What makes them leave again?

Here is a second example, from a company that was losing too many talented employees to other firms.

Goal	Reduce regrettable attrition from 14% to <10%
Problem	Not seeing reduction after trying things over last 5 months

This is a typical pain-point statement: we have tried stuff for five months with zero results. A situation like this is likely a good candidate for some reframing. Provided a solution exists, chances are that you'll find it by rethinking the problem rather than engaging in another five months of trial and error. In a preview of two of the reframing strategies we'll cover later, you could:

Rethink the goal. Is there a better goal to pursue? For example, instead of preventing attrition, can we do something to lure back our former employees from the competition after they leave? Can we find ways to get more out of the employees while we have them? Can we rethink our recruiting practices to target people who are less likely to leave? If people with a specific profile tend to quit before we have recouped the investment in training them, should we perhaps stop recruiting those people in the first place?

Examine bright spots. Instead of asking why people leave, we could ask why people *stay*. Looking at our top talent, what is it about our company that makes them say no to more lucrative or more exciting offers? Can we build on those strengths rather than trying to fix our weaknesses? Are there pockets of the business that do not see the same attrition? What might we learn from them? Or how about the people that we managed to recruit from "sexier" companies? What made those people join us? Can we get better at tapping into their personal networks of ex-colleagues, or otherwise turn them into informal ambassadors for our company?

5. With whom is the problem located?

One of the reasons you should use full sentences when describing the problem is that it allows you to spot small but critical details. One such detail is the presence or absence of words like *we, me,* or *they*—words that *locate* the problem.

Is the problem considered to be caused solely by other people? *The issue is that the staffers on the night shift are super lazy.* Or does the problem owner take some responsibility for the problem as well, like the team with the female role models did? ("We have not empowered . . .")

Is the issue framed in a way that relegates it to higher powers or pay grades, safely away from the problem owner's span of control? *We can't innovate unless the CEO gets serious about it.* In the most severe case, no recognizable human agency is found: *The problem is that our company's culture is too rigid.*

When we get to the reframing strategy called "Look in the Mirror" I'll share some advice on how to find more-actionable framings, including that of questioning your own role in creating the problem.

6. Are there strong emotions?

The statements we've analyzed so far are mostly neutrally worded. While not necessarily dispassionate, they didn't exactly convey a sense that epic emotions roared through the veins of the project teams. Compare those with this capital-letter problem statement from a manager who was, shall we say, not the happiest bunny in the forest:

INEFFICIENT PROCESSES CREATED
RANDOMLY BY PEOPLE
WITHOUT DESIGN MINDSETS

Here's a helpful piece of advice, shared with me by professor Steven Poelmans of Antwerp Business School: always dig into emotionally charged words. Words like *randomly*, or the slightly more subtle phrasing *people without design mindsets* (translation: idiots), suggest that you'll struggle to solve the problem on a logical or factual level alone.

Furthermore, assumptions that other people are stupid, selfish, lazy, or uncaring always deserve a second, deeper look. Often, what at first seems like complete idiocy is entirely sensible once you understand the reality of the other person. (In other cases, of course, your suspicions will turn out to be amply justified.) We'll go into more detail on this topic when we get to the reframing strategy called "Take Their Perspective."

7. Are there false trade-offs?

The most insidious problems present themselves as a trade-off, asking you to choose between two or more predefined options: *Do you want A or B?*

Poorly framed trade-offs are classic pitfalls for decision makers. The presence of multiple options creates the illusion of completeness and freedom of choice, even as the options presented may leave out much better alternatives.

In some situations, the people who frame the options are deliberately trying to steer you toward certain outcomes. The US statesman Henry Kissinger, for instance, famously joked about how bureaucrats that wanted to maintain the status quo would present a policy maker with three options: "Nuclear war, present policy, or surrender."

More often, though, the options you are presented with aren't the result of deliberate manipulation. Rather, they are simply assumed to be "natural" either-or trade-offs that everyone is facing. *Do you want high quality or low cost? Should your app be easy to use or have lots of customization options? Do you want wide reach or precise targeting in your marketing campaign?*

The problem-solving scholar Roger L. Martin and others have documented that creative thinkers tend to push back on such trade-offs. Where other people

do a cost-benefit analysis and pick the least painful option, expert problem solvers try to explore the issue in more depth and generate a new, superior option.

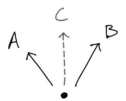

The starting point for that is the habit of trying to break the frame, asking *How is this choice framed? Are these the only options we have? What is the problem we're trying to solve?*

Here's the story of how one of the most impressive problem solvers I've met dealt with a false trade-off.

FEEDING THE HIPSTERS AT THE ROYAL PALMS

Serial entrepreneur Ashley Albert was in Florida. (It will tell you something about Ashley that she was in Florida to become certified as a judge of barbecue competitions.) During her visit, she noticed that some shuffleboard courts in a local park had been taken over by young hipsters—and they seemed to enjoy the game tremendously.

The encounter inspired Ashley and her business partner Jonathan Schnapp to start a similar venture,

The Royal Palms Shuffleboard Club, in Brooklyn's hipster-rich Gowanus neighborhood. Right away they faced a difficult choice: Should they serve food on the premises?

Anyone with experience in hospitality will tell you that this is a significant decision. Serving food is a huge hassle: there are health inspections, extra staff requirements, and lots of other administrative burdens. Even worse, it's not very profitable; drinks, especially alcohol, are where the money is. All this suggested that Ashley and Jonathan should stick to just serving beverages.

The problem was, the hipster is known to be a frequent forager. Without food at The Royal Palms, customers would stick around for only an hour or two. That wouldn't work. Ashley and Jonathan needed people to stick around for the entire evening, allowing them to benefit from the drinking that is so crucial to the hipster's prolonged courtship rituals.

Most entrepreneurs facing this dilemma end up biting the bullet and just accepting the administrative burdens that come with serving food. Others choose to avoid it, but are then stuck with a venue that's mostly empty around dinnertime. Ashley decided to see if she could find a third option. As she told me:

> Both of the options we faced were bad. So we started brainstorming on a different problem: *How can we get the benefits of serving food without the hassle that comes with it?* For various reasons, none

of the existing options, like using delivery services or partnering with a nearby restaurant delivery service, would have worked. But we kept mulling over the problem, and eventually we hit on a new idea— something that to my knowledge has never been done before.

Today, when you enter The Royal Palms, you'll see Brooklynites playing shuffleboard. There will be beards. There will be denim. There will be unique fashion choices. And in the right-hand corner of the club, you'll see something unusual: an opening into an adjacent garage that Ashley and Jonathan had built. In that garage, one of New York's ubiquitous food trucks is parked every night, feeding the hipsters.

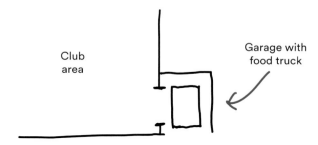

The solution is brilliant. As the food preparation is done entirely inside the food truck, using the driver's food permit, Ashley avoided the hassle of getting a food license. At the same time, the model gives Ashley and Jonathan the freedom to select different food types depending on the day and the season.

From the perspective of the food-truck owner, he or she had a captive audience that stuck around all evening, something that was especially attractive in the wintertime. And as Ashley and Jonathan made lots of money on the drinks, they could even offer a guaranteed minimum income to the food-truck owner in case it was a slow night.

Slow nights, however, haven't been a problem. As I write this, the club is highly profitable, and Ashley has just launched her second shuffleboard club in Chicago. Why Chicago? I asked her. "We need a place with bad weather so people want to stay inside."

A FINAL NOTE: SAVE THE DETAILS FOR LATER

The seven questions I shared here tend to be helpful, but they are far from the only ones you might ask. As you become more adept at reframing, you'll gradually add more such patterns to your mental library of problem-framing pitfalls.

Once you have done an initial review of the problem statement, the Frame step of the process is complete (remember the loop: Frame, Reframe, Move Forward). Before we start on the next step (Reframe), I want to make a note about what *not* to do at this stage. If you have some experience with goal setting, behavior change, or similar disciplines, chances are that some of the statements here made you itch to make them more specific and actionable. *What kind of goal is "healthier eating"? That's way too vague! A better goal would be "Eat at least three pieces of fruit every day, not including French fries."*

The instinct to be clearer about such details is a good one. As shown by decades of research on behavior change, people have much better chances of success if their goals are specific and measurable, and if the required behavior to reach them is clearly spelled out. Vagueness is the enemy of change.

However, at this point, there's a trap in giving in to your craving for specificity. If you are too quick to focus on the specifics, there is a significant risk that you will get lost in the details, and forget to question the overarching framing of the problem. You have to zoom out before you dive in: don't tinker with the specifics of the statement before you are fairly confident that you are looking at the right problem. That's what we'll look at next as we delve into the first of the five specific reframing strategies.

frame the problem

Before you can reframe a problem, you first have to frame it, giving you something to work on. To do so:

- Ask, "What problem are we trying to solve?" This triggers the reframing process. You might also ask "Are we solving the right problem?" or "Let's revisit the problem for a second."

- If possible, quickly write a problem statement, describing the problem in a few sentences. Keep it short, and use full sentences.

- Next to the statement, list the main stakeholders: Who is involved in the problem?

Once you have the first framing, subject it to a quick review. Look for the following in particular:

- **Is the statement true?** Is the elevator actually slow? Compared to what? How do we know this?

- **Are there self-imposed limitations?** At TV2, the team asked "Where can we find money?" instead of assuming it had to come out of their own budget.

- **Is a solution "baked into" the problem framing?** Often, problems are framed so that they point to a specific answer. This is not necessarily bad, but it's important to notice.

- **Is the problem clear?** Problems don't always present as problems. Often, you are really looking at a goal or a pain point in disguise.

- **With whom is the problem located?** Words like *we*, *me*, and *they* suggest who may "own" the problem. Who is *not* mentioned or implicated?

- **Are there strong emotions?** Emotional words typically indicate areas you should explore in more depth.

- **Are there false trade-offs?** Who defined the choices you are presented with? Can you create a better alternative than the ones presented?

Once you have completed the initial review, step 1 (Frame) is done, setting you up to reframe the problem.

look outside the frame

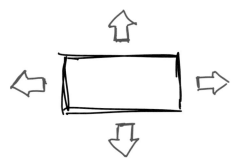

New York

Le Havre

Our ship

In the 19th century, the French mathematician Édouard Lucas posed a problem to some of his colleagues. The problem required no math skills and could be solved in less than a minute, and yet, none of his colleagues got it right.

Can you do better than the professional mathematicians? And just for good measure, this is not a trick question. You don't have to creatively reinterpret the words, turn the book upside down, or look for secret writing by dipping the page in lemon juice.

Don't read beyond this page until you are ready for the answer. (And if you can't be bothered to think it through in detail, just make a quick guess.)

The New York–Le Havre problem

The shipping company Bonjour operates a direct sailing route between New York and the French city Le Havre, with one departure each day in both directions. Specifically, every day at noon in New York, a ship sails to Le Havre, and simultaneously in Le Havre, a ship sails to New York. The crossing takes exactly seven days and seven nights in either direction.

The question is: If you leave New York on a Bonjour ship today, **how many other Bonjour ships will you pass at sea** before you arrive in Le Havre? You should count only the company's ships, and only the ones met at sea (meaning not in the harbor).

———————

Ready for the solution?

Some people guess either six or eight ships. After some careful thinking, though, most people conclude it must be seven ships—so if that was your answer, you're in excellent company.

Sadly, you're also wrong, because the correct answer is none of those—it is thirteen ships. Yes, thirteen. I'll explain in a minute.

The danger of a limited frame

The New York–Le Havre problem illustrates a common pitfall in problem solving: the danger of framing the problem too narrowly.

In short, we don't come to problems with a neutral view of the situation. On the contrary: in messy situations, it's as if your subconscious mind immediately draws a frame around a specific part of the problem before passing it on to your conscious self.

This first framing carries profound consequences. Everything *within* the frame is carefully scrutinized. Everything outside the frame, however, receives zero attention. In fact, because the framing process is largely subconscious—researchers have used the term "automatic"—we usually aren't even aware that we're not seeing the full picture.

Here's how that plays out in the New York–Le Havre problem.

Counting ships

Most people think through the problem more or less like this:

- Our trip takes seven days and nights, so we can figure out that a total of eight ships leaves Le Havre in that period. (One way to check this is to list the weekdays—you'll see a drawing of that on the next page.)

- We must meet all of those ships at sea, except for the 8th and final ship. That one launches just as we arrive in the harbor, so we don't count it, for a final answer of seven ships.

The calculation is correct, but it is also incomplete: we've missed the ships that sailed before our departure and are *already at sea* when we leave New York. The incomplete framing is shown on the next page, followed by the correct framing.

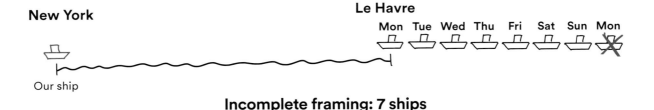

New York

Le Havre

Mon Tue Wed Thu Fri Sat Sun Mon

Our ship

Incomplete framing: 7 ships

New York

6 ships already at sea

Le Havre

Mon Tue Wed Thu Fri Sat Sun Mon

Our ship

Correct framing: 13 ships

Now, if you got it right, congratulations! A certain level of smugness and gloating is entirely in order. But if you got it wrong—and most people do—you should pause and reflect: *Why did you miss those six ships?* After all, it's not as if the challenge was presented in a completely innocuous context. You're reading a book on problem solving whose main point is that we don't frame problems correctly. With a setup like that, you *know* that there's a catch somewhere.

To understand why people get it wrong, it's necessary to realize that there is more at play than the unconscious framing effect. Significantly, with the New York–Le Havre problem, there are also highly "visible"

problems to ponder *inside* the frame, attracting the attention of our problem-crunching minds. Inspecting the initial framing, our minds are immediately drawn to questions like, *Hmm, is it seven or eight ships that launch during the week? How about the last one, I guess we meet that one in the harbor? Maybe I should count them, just for good measure. [Pulls out trusty fingers; starts counting.]*

Because there are some evident issues to grapple with inside the frame, we happily jump into thinking about those, while forgetting to ask if there are parts of the problem that we're not paying attention to at all.

The strategy: look outside the frame before you dive in

How do expert problem solvers avoid this trap? They deliberately avoid delving into the details of what's in front of them. Instead, they mentally "zoom out" and examine the larger situation, asking questions like, *What's missing from the current problem statement? Are there elements we're not considering? Is there anything outside the frame that we are not currently paying attention to?*

The habit of zooming out is used by experts in many different fields. In a study of expert designers, for instance, the design scholar Kees Dorst found that when working with clients, the expert designers "do not address the core paradox head-on, but tend to focus on issues around it. They search the broader problem context for clues."

Doctors do the same. As described in Lisa Sanders's book *Every Patient Tells a Story* (an excellent introduction to diagnosis in medicine), good doctors don't just focus on the stated ailment. They take a holistic view of the patient, their symptoms, and their history. In so doing, those doctors spot clues other doctors have missed, sometimes for years or decades.

Experts in operations science also practice zooming out. Inspired by the influential discipline called systems thinking, problem-solving experts in areas like manufacturing and workplace safety are trained to look beyond the immediate cause of an incident, searching for higher-level, systemic causes. *Yes, the dog ate your homework. But who left the homework in her bowl, sprinkled with dog chow?*

All of those approaches share the central concept of looking outside the frame before delving into the visible details. Here are four tactics that can prevent you from framing the problem too narrowly.

1. LOOK BEYOND YOUR OWN EXPERTISE

In his 1964 book *The Conduct of Inquiry*, the philosopher Abraham Kaplan coined what he called "the law of the instrument": "Give a small boy a hammer, and he will find that everything he encounters needs pounding."

Kaplan's delightfully memorable law came not from studying the feral children of carpenters but from his observations of scientists. Specifically, he found that scientists often framed a problem to match whatever techniques they were most proficient in.

They are not the only ones. Most people have a tendency to frame problems to match their own "hammer," hewing to the tools or analytical perspectives they favor. In some cases, that default solution simply doesn't work, which possibly—eventually—leads them to reconsider their approach. A potentially worse outcome, though, is when the favored solution does work, but by unthinkingly defaulting to their hammer, they fail to spot a much better way forward.

Here is an example from my work with a team of senior executives in Brazil. The team was asked to provide their CEO with ideas for improving the market's perception of their company's stock price.

Drawing on their financial expertise, the team quickly listed the various levers that influenced their stock price: the P/E ratio forecast, the debt ratio, earnings per share, and so on. Of course, none of this was news to the CEO, nor were these factors particularly easy to influence, leading to mild despondency on the team. But when I prompted the executives to zoom out and consider what was missing from their framing of the problem, something new came up.

(If you want to try and guess along, pause here and consider what the team came up with. Here's a hint: the insight came from an HR executive.)

———————

The HR exec asked, "Who talks to the analysts?" When external financial analysts called the company asking for information, they were typically put in touch with slightly more junior leaders—none of whom had received training in how to talk to analysts. As

soon as this point was raised, the group knew they had found a new potential recommendation for the CEO.

Area of expertise
All the financial levers
that affect our stock price

Who talks to the analysts
when they call us?

The story also illustrates the power of inviting outsiders into the reframing process. Since the stock price issue clearly seemed to be a financial problem, it might have been tempting to include only finance-savvy people in the meeting. The decision to include the HR executive (who was not a finance expert) brought a more people-oriented lens to the problem, allowing the team to look beyond the finance framing.

Merely having outsiders in the room isn't always sufficient, however. You have to actively invite them to come up with alternative framings. The strategy of zooming out and asking what's missing is one powerful way of doing so.

Letting go of your hammer

A quick remark on Kaplan's law of the instrument: it's not necessarily bad to have a default solution. Yes, there are situations in which blindly going with your default is problematic—for example, when you have only one shot at getting things right, or when your go-to solution can potentially cause harm when wrongly applied.

Except for these scenarios, though, it's not always a mistake to reach for the hammer you know best. On the contrary, we often have a preference for a specific tool precisely because it has worked well in the past, on most of our problems. Facing an unknown problem, it can be entirely logical to start with the tool you know best.

The real mistake happens when you keep using the hammer even after it's clear that it's not working. *My spouse is never ready to leave the house on time, no matter how much I yell at them. Hmm, maybe I should try some more yelling next time. The first fifty failures could have been statistical aberrations.*

If the problem you are facing is one you've repeatedly failed to solve with your preferred solution, then there's a good chance you need to reframe the problem. As the crime writer Rita Mae Brown put it: "Insanity is doing the same thing over and over again, but expecting different results."

2. LOOK TO PRIOR EVENTS

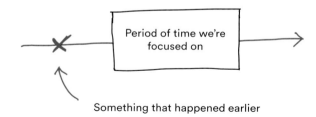

Something that happened earlier

Consider how you would respond to this situation:

Your teenage daughter comes back from school early, visibly upset. When you ask what's going on, she explains that she got into a shouting match with her teacher. The fight escalated to a point at which your daughter stormed out of the class. This is not like her: she's normally fairly well-behaved.

What questions would you ask your daughter to better understand the issue?

In situations like these, parents typically zoom in on the "visible" details: "How did the fight start? What did your teacher say? How did you respond? Why did that make you so upset?" Based on this granular analysis of the conversation, conclusions are drawn. *My daughter is becoming more rebellious; I guess she's a typical teenager after all.* Or maybe the blame shifts toward the teacher: *As the adult in the room, shouldn't he have been capable of handling the situation better? The school really needs to find better teachers!*

If you ask professionally trained school counselors, however, they will likely ask your daughter a different question: "Did you remember to eat breakfast this morning?" Surprisingly often, the difference between a civilized discussion and a huge fight lies in whether the people involved are running on an empty stomach. (Another popular variation is getting too little sleep.)

Like the ship counting problem, the breakfast example shows that you can sometimes shed new light on problems by noticing what happened before the slice of time you are currently focusing your attention on.

- What happened last time one of our employees tried to innovate?

- Which solutions did our client try to apply before coming to us?

- What happened to the last group of teenagers that rented this remote cabin in the woods?

The approach can be overdone, of course. Go too far back, and you end up contemplating deep historical factors that are hard to change. Still, consider whether you are framing the problem too narrowly from a time perspective.

3. LOOK FOR HIDDEN INFLUENCES

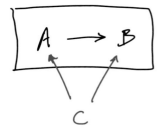

Hidden factor

If you ask an academic about logical pitfalls, you'll probably hear the phrase *mistaking correlation with causation*. Just because two things tend to occur together doesn't necessarily mean that one actually causes the other. Often, there is a third, underlying factor that's the real culprit. (Scientists call this a "confounding variable.") Here's an example.

What did the marshmallow test really show?

If you read popular science books, chances are you have already heard about the marshmallow test. In the experiment, Stanford psychologist Walter Mischel and his team put young kids in front of a marshmallow, one at a time, and told them, "If you refrain from eating this marshmallow for fifteen minutes, I'll give you a second marshmallow." And then they left the room and secretly watched what happened.

Mischel and his colleagues argued that the kids' ability to delay gratification was strongly predictive of their success as adolescents. Kids that resisted the temptation went on to become high-achieving, healthy young men and women. The low-willpower kids, not so much: they were less healthy and fared less well on a series of other measures too.

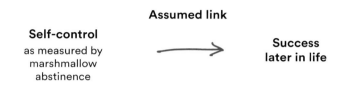

Assumed link

Self-control
as measured by marshmallow abstinence

Success later in life

Lesson learned: to make kids succeed, teach them willpower. Only, was that really what the study showed?

According to a recent study by Tyler Watts, Greg Duncan, and Haonan Quan, there is more to the story. Mischel and his colleagues had run the original study on 90 preschoolers, all of them from Stanford's campus. In the new study, Watts and his colleagues tested the theory on 900 children—and, crucially, they made sure to include children from less privileged backgrounds.

The result: It wasn't really about willpower. It was about money.

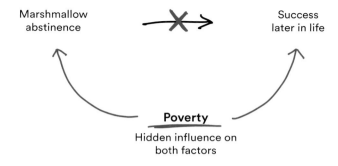

Marshmallow abstinence

Success later in life

Poverty
Hidden influence on both factors

The full explanation is nuanced, but here's the essence of it: Poor kids gobbled down the marshmallow faster because they had grown up in environments in which food might not be around tomorrow, and in which the grown-ups couldn't always keep their promises. Better-off kids, in comparison, were used to a more predictable future, one in which food was never scarce—and they knew from experience that adults generally kept their promises.

When the researchers factored this in, the link between marshmallow abstinence and future success became much less clear. If you want to help kids succeed, it's not necessarily about teaching them to delay gratification; it is about improving their socioeconomic conditions.

Here's a business example of finding hidden causal factors, shared with me by a finance executive we'll call Pierre. Pierre was asked to look into the interview process at his company, a major bank. The bank had a great brand and received lots of job applications from very talented people. However, many of the candidates the bank interviewed ultimately chose not to work there.

Initially, the team examined several factors: *Were the interviews too grueling? Were the pay packages not competitive? Did it matter, perhaps, who conducted the interviews from the bank's side?* None of those theories seemed to explain the pattern.

The mystery was solved only once Pierre looked outside the frame and found a hidden factor: the interviews with high rejection rates all took place *in the bank's old office building.* The candidates who were interviewed in the bank's new, more modern building, in comparison, loved the firm and generally made it their first choice. From that point onward, candidates were shown the old offices only after they had signed the contract and the bank vault had clanged soundly shut behind them.

4. LOOK FOR NONOBVIOUS ASPECTS OF THE SITUATION

The last two tactics I covered, looking for prior events and hidden influences, are really two different versions of the same thing—namely a search for causal factors.

Causes like those are not the only kind of elements that can be "hidden" outside the frame. Sometimes, finding the nonobvious solution hinges on thinking carefully about the properties of an object or a situation. Consider this classic challenge from the world of problem solving.

The light bulb problem

There are three light bulbs in the basement of your new house, but for some reason, the switches are located on the ground floor—and they aren't labeled. You have a sore knee, so you'd prefer to minimize the number of times you have to use the stairs. The question is: How many trips do you have to make into the basement to figure out which switch works with which light? For the record, the lights all work, each switch affects only one light bulb, and all three light bulbs are turned off when you start.

Pause here if you want to try to solve this.

———————————

If you gave it a bit of thought, you probably realized that you can do it in two trips. The third trip is unnecessary, as you can figure out the last match by a process of elimination. So far, so good.

But—there is also a way to solve it in one trip. Can you figure out how? Again, this is not a trick question, and it doesn't involve crazy stuff like drilling holes, tweaking the wires, or setting up elaborate systems of mirrors. The solution is simple and realistic and does not involve items or people that aren't mentioned in the problem statement.

Give it a try—but be warned: this one is harder to figure out. If you need a hint, I can tell you that the one trip solution relies on a nonobvious feature of one of the things that are involved. Think about what other properties a light bulb has besides emitting light.

The one trip solution

Here is the one trip solution to the light bulb problem:

1. Turn on two of the switches.

2. Wait one minute.

3. Turn one switch off again.

4. Go downstairs and *feel* the two unlit light bulbs. One of them will be warm to the touch.

If you are like most people, you found this solution to be a lot less obvious than the two-trip solution. And yet, everybody knows that light bulbs get warm when they are turned on—so why is this solution so much harder to find?

Frames allow us to see . . .

Because our subconscious mind tries to be as efficient as possible when it frames a problem—some researchers call the brain a cognitive miser—it allows only what it deems the most essential features to be included in the framing.

When mulling over the light bulb problem, for instance, you probably didn't stop to imagine the color of the wallpaper or whether it was summer or winter. Neither of those things seemed to have relevance for solving the problem, and so, quite sensibly, your mind simply didn't bother to think about them. Instead, it created a simplified representation of the problem— that is, a mental model—that you then started playing around with, throwing switches and whatnot until you found a solution.

. . . and frames blind us

This simplification is a good thing. Without the ability to quickly zoom in on the essential parts of a problem, we would be stuck thinking endlessly about wallpaper, to the delight of house decorators everywhere. But it also means that potentially useful elements or properties of the real world get left out.

A contributing factor is something called functional fixedness, which describes our tendency to focus only on the most common uses for things (light bulbs create light) and overlook less obvious uses (light bulbs can be used to create heat).

To identify such hidden aspects, ask questions like:

- What objects are involved in the situation?

- What other properties do they have? Can they be used in nontraditional ways?

- What else do we have available?

Here's a simple example of how a problem got solved by identifying and drawing on a hidden facet of the situation.

Imagine that you work as a parking attendant at Disneyland, managing the giant parking lot outside the theme park. Every day, more than ten thousand families arrive, park their cars, and head for the entrance.

Different areas of the massive lot are clearly marked so that people can find their vehicles when they head home: *Our car is in the Donald Duck zone, section 7B.* But every week, about four hundred sunbaked families, dazed by the experience and burdened by overstimulated kids in mouse ears, manage to forget where they left their car. How could this problem be solved?

A first observation might be that this type of problem has probably been solved before. (This is the essence of the "bright spots" strategy, which we'll cover later.) If you look at delivery services like FedEx or perhaps container facilities in commercial harbors, you'll find a number of solutions that use GPS tracking, license-plate scanning, and similar technologies.

Those would be expensive solutions here. Might there be a smarter solution that uses what's available and doesn't require new technology?

Yes. The parking attendants at Disney realized that there was one piece of information that people generally did remember, even if they forgot the parking-lot number: their arrival time. As the journalist Jeff Gray put it in the Canadian newspaper *The Globe and Mail*: "Disney staff simply write down the times that each row of the lot fills up in the morning. As long as customers know when they arrived, Disney staff can find their cars."

If you chose to work on your own problems as part of reading this book, now is the time to get to work. Pull out your written problem statements and try to apply the tactics to one or more of them. (It's up to you to decide how much time to spend on this before moving on.)

If you didn't choose to work on your problems, simply treat the next two pages as a chapter refresher, and ignore all instructions to review your problem statements.

look outside the frame

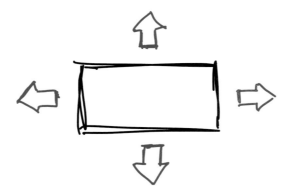

For each problem, remember to look outside the frame:

- Don't get caught up in the visible details.

- Think about what might be missing from your current framing of the problem.

Once you have done a general review, try to apply the four tactics described in the chapter, summarized here.

1. Look beyond your own expertise

Remember the law of the hammer: we tend to frame problems so that they match our preferred solutions. In Brazil, the finance people focused on the financial metrics of the stock price, overlooking the communications aspect.

Consider the following:

- What is your own favorite "hammer," meaning the type of solution you are good at applying?

- What type of problem does your hammer match?

- What if the problem was not such a problem: What else could it be?

2. Look to prior events

Recall the shouting match with the teacher in which a prior event may have caused the issue: "Did you eat breakfast this morning?"

Consider:

- How are you framing the problem from a time perspective?

- Did something important happen before the period of time you are looking at?

- For that matter, is there something after the time period that you missed? For instance, do people act a certain way because they fear a future outcome?

3. Look for hidden influences

Remember the marshmallow test and how the researchers overlooked the influence of poverty. Or think about how Pierre figured out the influence his bank's office building had on recruiting.

Consider:

- Are there stakeholders whose influence you're missing?

- Are there higher-level, systemic factors at play that influence the people involved?

4. Look for nonobvious aspects of the situation

Remember the light bulb problem, in which a less salient quality—that light bulbs emit heat—led to a more efficient solution than the one most people come up with.

- Are there nonobvious aspects of the problem or the situation that you could look into?

- Do you have data that can help you, or other things that are already available to us?

- How is functional fixedness affecting you?

Finally, are there *other* things "outside the frame" that you are not paying attention to? Incentives? Emotions? People or groups you have forgotten about? Briefly consider this, and then move on.

chapter 5

rethink the goal

WHY GOALS NEED TO BE QUESTIONED

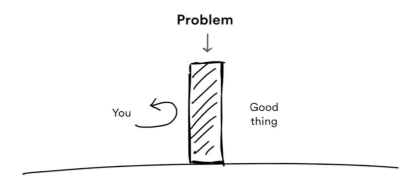

We often think of problems as obstacles: annoying things that stand in the way and prevent us from reaching something we want, such as money, happiness, or sweet, sweet revenge.

The problem-as-obstacle model feels intuitively right: we've all experienced being held back by a bureaucratic system, an uncooperative colleague, or some stupid set of antibribery laws. But there's a subtle trap in that way of thinking. Putting focus on the obstacle—how do we get around it?—prevents us from questioning a more important thing: the goal we're trying to reach.

In fact, most goals enjoy a strange immunity from scrutiny. Take your pick: Beating the competition. Growing the business. Driving innovation. Being promoted into a leadership role. All of these things are unthinkingly assumed to be appropriate aims, worthy of pursuit. The same goes outside of work for things like getting an education, finding a partner, and buying a home. Goals like these are deeply entrenched in our cultural narratives—and as a result, we often forget to question them.

It's not that the above-mentioned things are in reality bad and should be desperately avoided. In most cases, they *are* in fact good. But not always.

Sometimes, the key to radical breakthroughs is not to analyze the obstacle but to ask a different set of questions:

- *Are we pursuing the right goal?*

- *And is there a better goal to pursue?*

This is the essence of *rethinking the goal*. Consider the following story of a leader we'll call Mateo.

Finding a better goal

When Mateo took over the leadership of the review team, they were working hard to achieve an important and rather ambitious goal set by their old leader: *We need to cut our response time in half.*

The review team managed an important central database for their business. Every day, lots of other people inside the company would send various small change requests to the team. After making sure the change was okay, the team would apply it, essentially acting as a clearinghouse for the database.

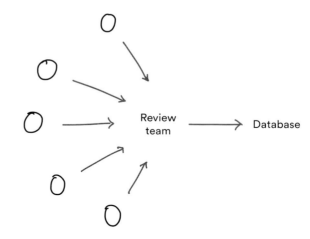

In the early days of the company, the review process had worked well. But as the company grew and the change requests multiplied, the team started being overloaded, to the point where all changes were subject to a two-week wait before being carried out.

To address the problem, the team's old leader had gathered his people and set a key goal for them to achieve:

> *Our current turnaround time is not acceptable. We need to make our team twice as fast at processing requests, bringing it down to one week.*

This is a typical example of a well-defined stretch goal: the end state we want to achieve is crystal clear, and it's evident to everyone why it matters. Energized by the goal, the team got to work.

A few months later, the old leader left, and Mateo took over the team. At Mateo's briefing, the old leader had mentioned the project: *The team is well on its way to reaching our one-week target, so you can just leave them to it. They'll get there.*

Mateo could easily have let the work continue and declared victory when the goal was eventually reached. What he did, though, would ultimately create much better results:

> Everyone was working hard to make the team faster at handling requests. But was that necessarily the right goal to pursue? As I thought about it, I realized that the real goal wasn't the *team's* speed: it was about reducing the time it took *for the business* to make changes to the database. The old goal had a big assumption buried in it—namely that everything had to go through our team and be manually approved. Once we stepped away from focusing on our team, it became clear that there might be another way forward: letting the business make some of the simpler changes directly, without our involvement.

Enter direct access

With Mateo's new focus, the team started looking at the types of changes that were requested. As it turned out, about 80 percent of the requests were both simple and fairly safe to implement. So for those requests, the team came up with the idea of a direct-access in-terface that allowed people outside of Mateo's group to make changes on the fly, bypassing the review team entirely.

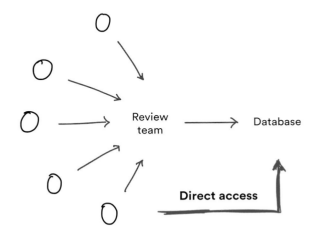

To be clear, the direct-access solution wasn't easy to implement. Mateo's team had to train the rest of the business in using it, and they had to get it done while also managing their daily workload. Mateo freed up time for his team by telling the other business units, "For a few months, we'll be *slower* than usual. But once we're done, we'll have a much better solution for you."

Mateo's promise held. A few months later, the two-week lag was completely removed for those 80 percent of requests that could be handled via the direct-access interface. Those could now be handled with no wait at all. And since the team now had more time, they also got faster at handling the changes that were too complex to be made via direct access. As a result of Mateo's decision to challenge the goal, the team vastly superseded the original objective of the one-week turnaround time.

––––––––––––

Mateo's story shows the power of rethinking your goals. By questioning what you are trying to achieve, you can sometimes find a way forward that creates dramatically better results. Here are five tactics you can use.

1. CLARIFY THE HIGHER-LEVEL GOALS

Goals don't really exist in isolation, as simple end-points to a journey: *get bacon, eternal bliss follows*. As the problem-solving scholar Min Basadur and others have argued, a better way to think about goals is to see them as part of a hierarchy or causal chain, going from lower- to higher-level "good things."

Take someone who seeks a promotion. Presumably, the promotion is not just an end in itself, but is a means to achieving something else the person wants—that is, one or more *higher-level goals*, such as making more money or becoming more respected. Here, you can see an example of how someone might describe the main higher-level goals behind their desire to get promoted.

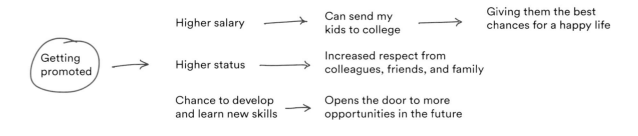

The drawing illustrates two important things. First, there's rarely only one thing we hope to gain from achieving a goal. Usually there are several different outcomes that matter to us.

Second, notice how some of the higher-level goals might also be means to an end. In the example, making more money isn't just a general goal to the person; it's the difference between sending both their kids to college versus having to tell one of them that they can't go. In operations science, these are sometimes called *distal goals*, to distinguish them from nearer or *proximate goals*. In advertising, a common expression is to "understand the benefit of the benefit" that a client hopes to attain. This is the same idea. Designers distinguish between features and benefits, negotiators between positions and interests, policy wonks between outputs and outcomes.

In any conversation about a problem, whether your own or someone else's, you should make sure to surface the higher-level goals. Do this by asking questions such as:

- What is your goal?

- Why is that goal important to you? Once you reach it, what will it help you achieve?

- Besides that, are there other important things that reaching the goal will help you do?

Sometimes, clarifying the higher-level goals can lead you directly to a creative solution. Take the following example from the field of negotiations research, shared by Roger Fisher, William Ury, and Bruce Patton in their classic book *Getting to Yes*.

The Camp David Accords

Famously, the idea of uncovering higher-level goals helped establish a peace treaty between Egypt and Israel back in 1978, when US President Jimmy Carter invited the parties to Camp David. As described in *Getting to Yes*, the conflict concerned a territorial dispute over the Sinai Peninsula. Sinai, originally Egyptian, had been under Israeli occupation since the Six Day War, in 1967. Egypt wanted all of its territory back. Israel wanted to keep at least part of it. The parties' stated goals—negotiators call them "positions"—were fundamentally incompatible, and as a consequence, every attempt at drawing a border had been rejected.

The stalemate was resolved once the parties' respective *interests* became clear. Egypt cared about *owning* the land. Israel, in contrast, wanted *security*: it was concerned about having Egyptian tanks parked right across the border, and saw Sinai as a buffer against invasion. From that difference, a solution was found: creating a demilitarized zone that belonged to Egypt but in which Egyptian armed forces couldn't be stationed.

As the story shows, making higher-level goals explicit is useful for conflicts involving more than one party.

However, the tactic is also relevant for problems that involve only one person—because people often *don't fully understand their own goals.* The psychotherapist Steve de Shazer has said that "clients often come with vague and/or mutually exclusive goals or goals which they cannot describe. In fact, the most difficult and confusing version of this is that some people do not know how they will know when their problem is solved."

When you clarify higher-level goals, it's typically enough to uncover the two or three most important objectives. Rarely has a good solution been rejected because someone's seventh-most-important goal wasn't met.

The same goes for moving "up" the hierarchy, meaning toward higher-level goals. The useful reframings tend to lurk within the first few levels of abstraction. Venture much farther and goals become so high-level as to be almost useless for reframing purposes. (They can still guide general decision making, though—involving, for example, personal values or corporate purpose statements.)

2. CHALLENGE THE LOGIC

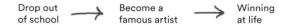

A goal map (like the promotion example) is more than just a list of good things. It's also a model of *how you think the world works,* complete with the key causal mechanisms you believe are in play. These causal links are important to surface, because sometimes, they're wrong.

The easy example is to consider teenagers, who we, their wise elders, can all agree are mistaken about pretty much everything. Take this mildly simplified model of career success:

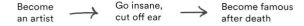

Most adults would probably delight in pointing out the logical leaps of this model, perhaps by highlighting how things worked out for, say, Van Gogh:

Become an artist → Go insane, cut off ear → Become famous after death

However, it's not just young people who sometimes have bad models of how the world works. Experienced professionals, too, can be held captive by bad logic—even when it comes to their own area of expertise. Here is an example of that, from Henrik Werdelin.

Rethinking the finance function:
Are longer payment terms better?

If you've ever sold a product or service to a large corporation, you are probably familiar with terms like *Net-30*, *Net-60*, and *Net-90*: they are payment terms, specifying how many days the company has to pay you what it owes.

From the big company's perspective, a Net-90 policy is like getting an interest-free loan for three months, so it's not surprising that large companies often use their power to push for longer payment terms, paying their suppliers as late as possible. Basically, most big-company finance people have something like this goal model in their heads:

The logic of the model seems pretty unassailable. But *is* it actually better? As Werdelin explained:

> If you take three months to pay your bills, you are effectively forcing the company to work only with big suppliers, because they are the only ones who have enough cash to get their money that late. Freelancers, who are often much cheaper, can't survive on those payment terms. So an across-the-board

Net-90 policy can actually lock your company into using only the most expensive vendors.

Following that logic, several of the big companies Werdelin advises have introduced a tiered payment system, getting them the best of both worlds.

To check for similar logical leaps, look at your goal model and ask:

- Are our key assumptions actually true? Does the stated goal necessarily lead to the outcome we ultimately want?

- Even if an assumption is generally true, are there special circumstances in which it doesn't apply? Do we need to refine or revise our thinking about how we win?

With this step in particular, it can help to have outsiders involved in the discussion. As one expert in sense-making, Anna Ebbesen, of Red Associates, put it:

> There can be a fine line between facts and assumptions. Sometimes, our assumptions are so heavily ingrained in our thinking that we mistake them for facts about the world. Other times, the assumption was originally a fact—but then something about the world changed, rendering it invalid. Our most fundamental assumptions are hard for us to see as such. You often need some kind of outside input to do it.

3. ASK IF THERE ARE OTHER WAYS TO ACHIEVE THE IMPORTANT GOALS

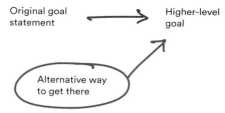

Once you know the higher-level goals, you can explore a central question: Is the immediate goal the best way to get there? Or are there other ways to achieve the outcome we really care about?

Take the personal goal outlined earlier, about the promotion. An important aim of being promoted is getting a "higher salary," so that you can achieve something that really matters, like paying for college for your kids.

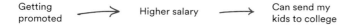

A first observation might be that the word *salary* is overly narrow: it limits our thinking by implying that cash has to come via a paycheck, when it's really about money in general. (Remember chapter 3's discussion of simple self-imposed limitations.) A more useful goal might be "set aside X dollars over the next five years."

That, in turn, allows you to look for other ways to achieve the goal besides the promotion. Here is an

illustration of a few alternative ways forward that might be worth exploring.

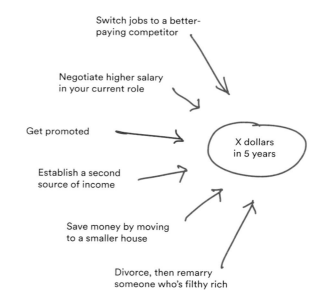

Here's a memorable real-world example of this tactic from Robert J. Sternberg, a major figure in creativity and problem-solving research.

How to escape a horrible boss

In his book *Wisdom, Intelligence, and Creativity Synthesized*, Sternberg tells the story of an executive who loved his job but hated his boss. The executive's contempt for his boss was so strong that he decided to contact a headhunter and look for a new job within the same industry. The headhunter explained that with the executive's strong track record, finding a similar job elsewhere should be easy.

The same evening, however, the executive spoke to his wife, who happened to be an expert on reframing. This led to a better approach. In Sternberg's words: "He returned to the headhunter and gave the headhunter his boss's name. The headhunter found a new job for the executive's boss, which the boss—having no idea of what was going on—accepted. The executive then got his boss's job."

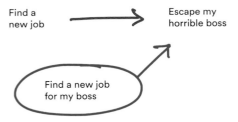

4. QUESTION OBVIOUS GOALS, TOO

Some goals seem so self-evidently good that it feels silly to question them. Who wouldn't want to make things faster, cheaper, safer, nicer-looking, or more efficient? But in fact, the very obviousness of these goals can lead us astray—because what might seem like a good goal in an isolated sense is not necessarily the right thing to do when you look at the bigger picture. Take the following example from Intel.

Most people know Intel from the processors in their computers. What is less known is the company's work for Stephen Hawking, the iconic theoretical physicist and wheelchair user. Ever since Intel cofounder Gordon Moore met Hawking at a conference in 1997, Intel had been updating the software on Hawking's wheelchair every two years, free of charge.

The most important part of that job was to improve the custom-designed text-to-speech computer that allowed the physicist to communicate with the world. In 1997, the system allowed Hawking to type only one to two words per minute, making conversation excruciatingly slow. Intel's team managed to increase the speed dramatically, using the kind of predictive text algorithms that we now know from our smartphones.

Some years later, when it became time for another update, the designer Chris Dame was part of Intel's team: "We were very proud to show Stephen a new version of the software that let him communicate even faster than the old model. So we were rather surprised by his reaction: *Can you make it slower?*"

As it turned out, Hawking was multitasking. While he composed a sentence, the other people in the room would naturally continue talking with him and each other, and Hawking liked to follow the conversation and occasionally make eye contact with people as he typed. The new and "improved" system didn't permit him to do that. It was so fast that Hawking felt "locked into" the computer until he had finished writing. At some point, more speed became a bad thing, even if it was the very quality that was the goal at the beginning.

The world is full of such counterintuitive examples. Those late-night TV shop commercials that look like they were produced decades ago? They are deliberately amateurish-looking, because that sells better than glitzy, high-production-value commercials. That long walk from your flight's arrival gate to the baggage-claim area? It gives the airline more time to get your baggage out so you spend less time wait-grumbling at the conveyor (something people dislike more than having to walk longer).

Authenticity and other bad things

Our failure to question goals is exacerbated because some words have only a positive connotation. Take *authenticity*. Who in their right mind wouldn't want to be more authentic? (*"Great presentation, Kate—but could you try to sound a bit more canned next time?"*) The very word tells us all you need to know about the desirability of attaining it.

And yet, authenticity, too, can be a bad goal to aim for. Take the transition into a new job as a leader. Stepping into a leadership role is by definition not natural to most people. As INSEAD professor Herminia Ibarra has pointed out, allowing yourself to experiment with new behaviors that might not at first feel "authentic" is in fact a core part of developing as a person. A blind adherence to the goal of authenticity can trap you in your past, static self.

Many other examples exist. Originality, for one, sounds like a great quality. But to risk-averse decision makers, *original* means untried, untested, and likely to go down in flames—consider, for example, the film industry's preference for sequels and remakes. (If you want to find investors for your new movie, you may be better off with "just different enough to avoid lawsuits.")

Outside of work, consider personal happiness as a goal. Is maximizing your own day-to-day happiness always a good idea? Martin Seligman, founder of the positive psychology movement, has argued that genuine well-being isn't just about having more positive emotions. A truly fulfilling life also involves pursuing hard-to-reach goals and having a positive impact on others—which may mean walking a harder road than the one between the fridge and the TV.

5. EXAMINE THE SUBGOALS AS WELL

Until now, we've focused on the higher-level goals. It's also worthwhile to look at *sub*goals, meaning the intermediate steps we believe will lead us to a goal.

In the example of getting a promotion, here's what the subgoals may look like:

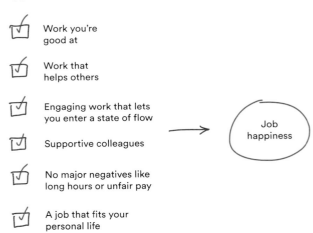

Just like your higher-level goals, the subgoals are part of your overall mental model of how the world works. Accordingly, the subgoals, too, can be wrong, incomplete, or in need of rethinking. Take this uncontroversial career ambition:

Getting a job that makes me happy

Before you read on, take a second to think about your own mental model with regard to this goal. What would you say are the main factors that make a job feel fulfilling? What should you be looking for when you make your next career move?

According to the British nonprofit initiative 80,000 Hours, founded by Benjamin Todd and Will MacAskill, most people think happiness at work comes from two things: high pay and low stress levels.

Research into what actually makes people love their jobs, though, points elsewhere. Based on a review of over sixty different studies of job satisfaction, Todd and MacAskill cite six factors that lead to professional happiness.

For both higher- and lower-level goals, first clarify and then challenge your assumptions to ensure that you are solving for the right goal.*

---

*As you may notice, it's somewhat arbitrary what you call a goal, a subgoal, and a higher-level goal. Don't put too much emphasis on the terminology; it is just a reflection of where in the hierarchy you happen to start. The important thing is to explore both "up" and "down" from the goal you initially choose to look at.

rethink the goal

Review your problem statements.

- Start by writing down the goal: *What would success look like? What is the goal (or goals) I am trying to achieve?*

- Then draw a goal map (like the promotion example) to clarify the higher-level goals.

- If you like, you can also map the subgoals at the same time. *What steps are necessary or helpful to achieve your goal?*

If you need more guidance in drawing the map, try to apply these questions to each listed goal in the map, based on Min Basadur's work:

- Surface higher-level goals by asking, *Why do we want to achieve this goal? What is the benefit? What is the goal behind the goal?*

- Surface subgoals by asking, *What is stopping us from reaching this goal?*

- Look for other goals as well by asking, *What else is important?*

Once you have drawn the map, do a quick review to see if any of the goals are defined too narrowly. (Remember the example of "I need a higher salary" versus "I need X dollars in five years.") Ask, *Are there any simple self-imposed limitations?* Make sure the framing of the goals doesn't imply a specific solution unless it's genuinely necessary.

Then try to apply the remaining tactics we covered in the chapter.

Challenge the logic

Recall how the finance teams weren't necessarily right about the benefits of Net-90 terms. Ask:

- Are our assumptions actually true? Does the immediate goal necessarily lead to the outcome we ultimately want?

- Even if it's generally true, are there special circumstances where it doesn't apply? Do we need to refine or revise our thinking about how we win?

Are there other ways to achieve the important goals?

Remember Robert Sternberg's story of the executive who used the headhunter to get his boss a different job instead of himself. Recall as well Lori Weise's story (from chapter 1): Instead of getting more shelter dogs adopted, can we help their families so that their dogs never enter the shelter system in the first place?

In a similar manner, ask:

- Are there better goals to pursue?

- Are there alternative ways of achieving the higher-level goal?

Question obvious goals, too

Are there any goals that sound so obviously good that they should not be questioned? Question them anyway—and be wary of words with positive connotations, such as *authenticity*, *originality*, and *safety*.

Examine the subgoals as well

If you haven't already, map the subgoals, and then subject them to the same scrutiny. What might you be wrong about? What might you be forgetting?

examine bright spots

THE POWER OF POSITIVE EXCEPTIONS

The start of Tania and Brian Luna's otherwise happy marriage was plagued by a recurring issue: they occasionally got into big fights about small things like cleaning, spending, or dog care. And while every couple fights sometimes, both Tania and Brian felt that their conflicts too often became needlessly bitter.

After it had happened a few times, they started analyzing the problem. Why did their fights get so bad? As Tania told me, "Our initial focus was on the how and the why. We looked at who said what, and we spent time focusing on deep things like values and how we were brought up."

Notice the pattern here. When it comes to people problems, we often default to seeking deep, historical explanations, perhaps inspired by Sigmund Freud: *It has to be something in our childhoods.*

Such a framing may well be true, but it's also difficult to do anything about. The same goes for the "values" framing: *We just have different values, honey. I value progress, and you value being an idiot. Glad we got that cleared up.* In Tania and Brian's case, those types of framings weren't helpful.

What did help was their analysis of a *positive exception.* As Tania explained,

> One day we had a conversation over breakfast about our budget—and it was so smooth and painless. The same topic that seemed impossibly complex and upsetting at night was easy after we slept and ate. That made us pause and rethink what was going on. We soon realized what most of our arguments had in common: they were happening after ten in the evening. We didn't fight because of our different

values. We fought because we were sleepy, hungry, and therefore cranky.

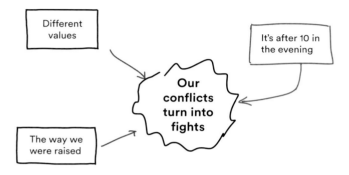

The reframing led Tania and Brian to institute what they call "The Ten O'Clock Rule."

> In short: we can't bring up any serious or contentious topics after ten in the evening. And if one of us tries to pick a fight, the other just says "ten o'clock!" and all bickering must stop. The rule has been our best problem-solving tool, and has gotten us through nearly a decade of a very happy marriage :-)

The story reinforces a key point of this book: often there are several ways to solve a problem. If Tania and Brian had chosen, say, to go into couples therapy, there's a decent chance they would have solved the problem, or at least found a way to cope with it. As it happened, they found a better way forward by paying attention to a different question: *When do we* not *have the problem? Are there any bright spots?*

The strategy: examine bright spots

The point of the bright spots strategy—a useful term coined by authors Chip and Dan Heath—is to look for situations or places where the problem is not as bad, or where it may even be entirely absent. Paying attention to such positive exceptions can give you a new perspective on the problem, and may even point you directly to a viable solution.

The origins of the bright spots approach can be traced to two fields. One is medicine. Doctors have long known the power of asking their patients, *Are there times where you don't feel as bad?*

The other is engineering, one of the first fields outside of medicine to create formal frameworks for problem diagnosis. Here, the strategy was popularized by Charles Kepner and Benjamin Tregoe in an influential 1965 book on root cause analysis, which taught problem solvers to ask, *Where is the problem not?* Since then, the bright spots question has become a staple of problem-solving frameworks everywhere.

With bright spots, the actual reframing is rarely complicated. The hard part is typically to *find* the bright spots—because sometimes, they are located in rather surprising places. Here are four questions to help you find them*:

1. Have you already solved the problem at least once?

2. Are there positive outliers in our group?

3. Who else deals with this type of problem?

4. Can we broadcast the problem widely?

1. HAVE YOU ALREADY SOLVED THE PROBLEM AT LEAST ONCE?

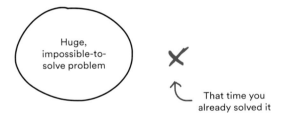

If you decided to go into therapy in the 1970s, chances are you and your therapist would continue to meet for years, spending session after session exploring your past: *And how about your mother's mother? What was*

---

*As with the rest of this book's strategies, I draw on a wide body of prior work in the area. For this chapter, I want to highlight my particular indebtedness to Chip and Dan Heath's excellent books *Switch* and *Decisive*. People familiar with their work will recognize that I've echoed some of their advice here.

her *deep-rooted defect?* The therapist was effectively like a cave diver, ready for round after round of spelunking into the innermost parts of your psyche.

In the early 1980s, a small group of therapists in Milwaukee discovered a different approach, now called *solution-focused brief therapy.* Led by Steve de Shazer and his wife, Insoo Kim Berg, the group noticed something astonishing: much like Tania and Brian with their effortless breakfast discussion, many of the group's clients *had already solved their own problem at least once.* Only unlike Tania and Brian, they hadn't really noticed the bright spot, and so had failed to learn from it.

In those cases, no cave diving was necessary. The job of the therapist was to guide the client in finding the bright spots and then encourage the client to reapply the same behavior. Using that approach, the Milwaukee group managed to help their clients move forward using an average of only eight therapy sessions.

How to find bright spots

To apply the Milwaukee group's insight to your own problems, do the following:

- Look to the past. Was there ever a time—even just once—when the problem didn't occur, or when it was less severe than usual?

- If so, examine the bright spot carefully. Are there any clues that can shed new light on the problem?

- If the analysis doesn't yield clues, can you try repeating the behaviors? Is it possible to recreate the circumstances that led to the bright spot?

- If you can't find a bright spot for your current problem, consider whether you have ever solved a *similar* problem? Might that provide some clues?

Three rules of thumb

As you look for bright spots in your past, keep these three guidelines in mind:

Seek unexceptional exceptions. If work causes you a lot of stress, recalling that time you took a four-month vacation isn't a terribly helpful bright spot. A more useful one would be closer to the situation in which the problem occurs. Was there a day recently when your work did not stress you out as much? What was different about that day?

Examine* really *positive exceptions too. Don't look only for the absence of problems. Also examine occasions when things were truly great. Was there a day you actually *gained* energy from work? Handling stress better, for instance, is not always about avoiding the things that cause stress. It can be just as much about adding more positive things to your day, giving you greater mental surplus to deal with the stress factors.

When did the problem occur but not matter? The absence of bad *effects* of a problem is also a bright spot. For the stress problem, you might ask: Was there a day when you got stressed but managed not to let yourself be as affected by it? What did you do differently?

In the world of hotels, for example, it's well known that you can't give hotel guests the perfect stay every time. Mistakes will happen: food orders arrive late, dry cleaning gets mixed up, room keys stop working at the most inconvenient time possible. However, such mistakes don't always have negative consequences. As the hotel executive Raquel Rubio Higueras told me:

> Normally it's not the mistake as such that makes a guest unhappy. What really matters is how the hotel staff handles the mistake. In some cases, if the staff reacts promptly and goes out of their way to fix it, guests will actually rate their stay *higher* than if the mistake had never occurred.

Long-term thinking in a law firm

Here is a business example from a lawyer named Anders. Every so often, Anders would meet with some of the other partners in his law firm to brainstorm on new initiatives: *How might we grow our business in the longer term?* Many of their ideas seemed promising, and everyone agreed that they were worth exploring.

Their good intentions didn't last long, though. To Anders's frustration, once the meetings ended, everyone—himself included—went back to focusing exclusively on short-term projects. As at many firms, the tyranny of the next quarter's results mercilessly trounced the partners' aspirations for the future, again and again.

When prompted to look for bright spots, Anders remembered one longer-term initiative that had gone forward. What was different about that one? That meeting, unusually, included not just partners but also an associate who was considered a rising star—and she ended up pursuing the idea.

That immediately suggested a course of action: include talented associates in future brainstorms. The associates felt privileged when invited to the strategic discussions, and unlike the partners, they had a clear short-term incentive to move on long-term projects—namely to impress the partners and gain an edge in the competition against their peers.

2. ARE THERE POSITIVE OUTLIERS IN OUR GROUP?

What if you don't have a bright spot in your own past? In that case, you should check if there are any in your immediate peer group:

- Our employee engagement numbers are terrible. *Then again, two of our leaders seem to be doing great.*

- Sales are down everywhere—*well, apart from this one small market where they grew by 5 percent.*

- My parents are *so* exhausting to deal with! *Except, my eight other siblings seem to get along with them pretty great.*

Even with really tough problems, given a large enough group, there are often some outliers who have found a way to cope with them. And as pioneers within the international aid community have shown, those outliers can be key in reframing the problem. Here's an example of that from the work of Jerry Sternin, one of the founders of the so-called positive deviance approach.

Getting illiterate parents to keep their kids in school

At one point, some members of Sternin's team worked with a group of teachers and school principals in the rural Misiones province of Argentina. The problem they faced had to do with dropouts: only 56 percent of children in the province completed their primary-school education (compared with a national average of 86 percent).

One big reason had to do with the parents, many of whom were both poor and illiterate. As they had never been schooled themselves, most of them didn't seem to care much about keeping their kids in school. Hectoring the parents about the importance of education for their kids' future didn't help. As the schools had very limited resources, most teachers didn't think there was much to be done.

Sternin's team knew that there was probably another angle on the problem—and that letting the teachers examine some bright spots could surface it. As they put it in their book *The Power of Positive Deviance*:

> The initial framing of the problem often turns out to be a placeholder. If experience teaches one lesson, it is that problem reframing usually occurs along the way. The surest way for a community to recognize a problem as its own is for people to frame it in their own words and ground it in their own reality.

To make that happen, Sternin's team presented the group with some interesting data: while most schools in the province had the same problem, there were three exceptions. Two schools retained 90 percent of their students, above the national average. A third school retained *100 percent*. None of the three schools had access to extra resources. What was going on?

The answer was rooted in teacher behavior. Across the province, most teachers treated the illiterate parents with condescension. At the bright spot schools, in contrast, teachers tried to engage with the parents—for instance, by creating annual "learning contracts" with them before the school year. That engagement led to an important insight: in some cases, what the kids learned in school could *directly benefit their parents here and now*. In the team's words: "As the children learned to read, add, and subtract, they could help

their parents take advantage of government subsidies and compute the amount earned from crops or interest owed at the village store."

This offered the teachers a different way to enlist the parents as partners. Keeping your kid in school wasn't just about giving the kid some vague advantage in the future (which can seem far off when you are poor). It could also be of clear, immediate value to the parents: *At the end of the year, if you help keep her in school, your daughter can help you with the accounts.*

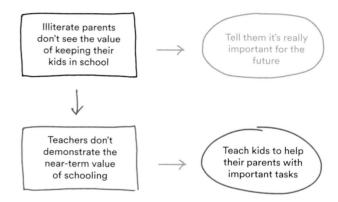

As a result of the insight, two of the school districts in the province decided to replicate the approach of the bright spot schools—and saw a 50 percent increase in their retention rates one year later.

To find similar bright spots in your peer group, ask: *Has anyone we know solved the problem—or at least found a better way to handle it?*

3. WHO ELSE DEALS WITH THIS TYPE OF PROBLEM?

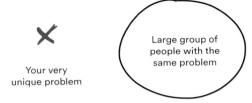

Your very unique problem

Large group of people with the same problem

When I give talks to cross-industry audiences, I often do a short exercise in which I ask people to pick a problem they face here and now. I then ask them to reframe it in small groups, working with people from outside their industry.

At the outset, most people don't see the point: *How would these people ever be of use to me? My problem is deeply unique and industry-specific. In fact, nobody has ever encountered anything like it in the history of, well, ever. That's five minutes of my life I'll never get back.*

One short discussion later, as I debrief the exercise, one of the groups will invariably say: "We discovered that we all have the exact same problem!"

They don't, of course. Problems are always unique in the specifics. But at the same time, once you look beyond the details, many problems share what the author and cognitive scientist Douglas Hofstadter calls a "conceptual skeleton"—that is, they are the same *type* of problem. That's what makes people say, "I have the same problem!"

When you're looking for bright spots, the specifics are often of secondary importance: you don't have to find an exact match for your problems. In fact, less is more: by defining your problem in *less* detail, you make it easier to find bright spots elsewhere. Here's Martin Reeves, head of Boston Consulting Group's Henderson Institute and a leading thinker on problem solving:

> You have to start with the details: What are the key observable features of this problem? But once you have that, you then have to step away from the details and conceptualize the problem, finding a more abstract way to express it. Doing that will allow you to ask, *Where else have we seen this kind of problem?*

This is a key step in Boston Consulting Group's problem-solving process, allowing the firm to look for solutions and bright spots in other industries. To do the same, ask:

- What type of problem am I facing? How can we think about it in broader, more general terms?

- Who else deals with this type of problem? What might we learn from them?

Here's a story of a team that used this approach.

Pfizer solves a cross-cultural problem

While working at the medical giant Pfizer, Jordan Cohen created a successful internal service called pfizerWorks. It allowed Pfizer's employees to out-source the boring parts of their work—such as data vetting, slide preparation, and market research—to teams of virtual analysts.

Some of the analysts that pfizerWorks relied on were located in Chennai, India—and uniquely for this type of service, the analysts would interact directly with Pfizer's employees in the United States and elsewhere, rather than communicating through a central office.

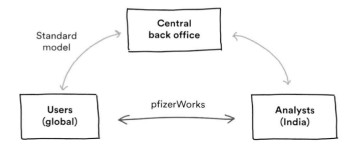

The model made pfizerWorks much faster and more cost-effective—but it also gave rise to a big problem. As Seth Appel, a member of Jordan's team, told me:

A Pfizer employee in New York would email the Chennai team with an inquiry about a report, only the person she was seeking to speak to wasn't in the office. Now, if you were emailing someone who was familiar with Western communication norms, you'd get a politely phrased answer back: "Dear Kate, thanks for your message. I'm sorry to say that Santosh, the lead on your project, is not currently in the office, but I will make sure he responds promptly when he returns tomorrow at 8 a.m. your time."

Instead of that, though, Kate would get a one-line reply saying: *Santosh is not in right now.*

That kind of reply created much anger and confusion: *What kind of message is this? Is no one on top of my report? Will I get it on time? Do I really need to write back just to even hear if he'll get the message?* As the sociologist and key reframing thinker Erving Goffman pointed out as far back as the 1960s, cultural norms are pretty much invisible—right until you break them.

How could the problem be solved? Looking for bright spots within their own industry didn't help: at the time, nobody let analysts deal directly with the users. So Jordan and Seth framed it on a more conceptual level:

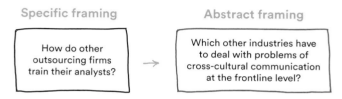

If you want to guess along, pause here and try to consider the question—and what type of solution they ultimately found.

———————

Seth and Jordan found a bright spot in the hospitality industry. Large international hotel chains that were based in India needed to staff their front desk and concierge services with people who could communicate both with locals and with people from lots of different cultures.

Next, Seth and Jordan could have figured out how the hotels trained their front-desk staff, and then used the same approach with their analysts. Instead, they struck on an even simpler approach: *hire people directly from the hotels*. As Seth told me,

> Our team needed to have two main skills: analytical skills to do the job, and then cultural skills to handle communications. So instead of hiring skilled analysts and then teaching them how to communicate, we realized it was easier to hire people who were already culturally fluent, and then teach them the necessary analytical skills. So that's what we did—and it worked.

4. CAN WE BROADCAST THE PROBLEM WIDELY?

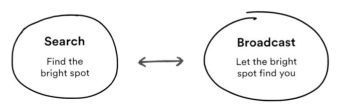

The approach we just covered has one clear drawback: you need some idea of where to look. Once Jordan's team asked *who else has problems with cross-cultural communication*, the connection to big hotels wasn't too difficult to spot. But what if the useful bright spots reside in an industry you've never heard of?

In that case, there's another approach you can take: **broadcast your problem**. As research has shown, by sharing your problem widely and getting it in front of different groups, you increase the chances that someone will connect you to a bright spot you didn't know about. Here are some simple ways to do it:

- In your next lunch break, sit down with people from other departments and share your problem. (Ask them what problems they face, too.)

- Describe the problem on your company's intranet or similar in-house channels.

- Talk to friends who work in other industries (assuming the problem isn't confidential).

- If the problem can be shared in public, consider using social media to solicit input.

For bigger problems, especially within R&D, more advanced broadcasting options exist as well. Some online problem-solving platforms allow you to share your problem (for a fee), putting it in front of communities of "solvers" from all over the world. Others can connect you to expert networks or can offer to run a public idea competition for you. Before you consider those, though, try the simpler versions first. As the following story shows, you don't always need a lot to make a difference.

The case of E-850

When researchers at the global science company DSM invented a new form of glue called E-850, it looked like a clear winner. It worked better than most competing products, and it was more ecologically friendly, making it very attractive to DSM's customers.

But a problem emerged. A key application for E-850 was to glue thin layers of wood together to create the kind of laminated boards used as table surfaces. When the researchers tried to apply a coating to the boards that were glued with E-850, the laminate would start fraying at the edges.

The glue couldn't be brought to market before the problem was solved. Unfortunately, it was a difficult problem. After two years, the R&D team still hadn't solved it.

Then, the DSM employees Steven Zwerink, Erik Pras and Theo Verweerden decided to try broadcasting the problem. To make things easy, they created a PowerPoint deck that described the problem and shared the deck on various social media channels. To encourage people to help, they offered a €10,000 reward for the solution—a tiny amount compared with the potential gains if DSM could get the product to market.

Two months later, the team published a second deck with a happy announcement: a number of people had responded to their challenge and the specific input from five people, when taken together, allowed the researchers to find a solution.* As a result, DSM could finally move forward and put E-850 on the market, where it became a great success.

Incidentally, the DSM case also illustrated that solutions might be closer than you think. Of the five people that contributed to the solution, *three of them worked for DSM*. One was a scientist. The second was a key account manager. The third was an attorney trainee in the company's patent office. Broadcasting your problem allows input to surface from unexpected places.

---

*As it happened, the solution involved reframing the problem. I haven't described the details here, as they are a bit technical, but if you are a lamination aficionado—and really, who isn't?—you can read all about it in the endnotes.

Three tips for broadcasting problems

When broadcasting a problem, here are three quick pieces of advice from Dwayne Spradlin, founder of the problem-solving website InnoCentive:

- **Avoid technical language.** Make sure people can understand it even if they don't work in your industry.

- **Provide lots of context.** Why is the problem important to solve? What are the core constraints? What have you already tried?

- **Don't overspecify the solution.** Instead of writing, say, "We need a cheaper way to drill wells," write "We need to provide clean drinking water to 1.2 million people" (which might not involve wells).

———————

The strangest thing about the bright spots strategy is that it's necessary in the first place. As you've seen, many bright spots reside in places we already know about—and some can be found *in our own past* (this idea is still quietly mind-boggling to me). Somehow, you would think that we'd be better at spotting them automatically.

And yet, we aren't. We all suffer from a phenomenon called *negativity bias*, scientific shorthand for the simple idea that people tend to pay more attention to bad things than to good things. When confronting problems, we're wired to focus on what's going wrong, thereby failing to learn from what's working well.

The bright spots strategy is meant to fix that. By flipping the script and directing your attention to the positive—what works?—you can find new ways forward. Just remember to use it.

examine bright spots

Revisit your own problem statements. For each problem, consider if there are any bright spots.

Have you already solved the problem at least once?

People often struggle with problems *they have already solved*. Via their painless discussion over breakfast, Tania and Brian Luna realized that their fights were caused in part by their timing. With that in mind, consider if there was ever a time—even just once:

- When you didn't have the problem

- When the problem was less severe

- Or when the problem happened, yet the usual negative impact didn't occur

Is there anything you can learn from these bright spots? If not, can you potentially recreate the behaviors or circumstances that led to the bright spot—basically, doing more of what works?

Are there positive outliers in our group?

Recall the story of the illiterate parents in Argentina's Misiones district: by studying three "outlier" schools, the schools found a better way to frame the problem of parental involvement.

- Is there anyone in your peer group that has solved the problem? Can you find out what they're doing differently?

Who else deals with this type of problem?

To find bright spots in other industries, remember Martin Reeves's point about describing the problem in more abstract terms and how that helped the pfizer-Works team find a bright spot in the hotel industry. In the same way:

- How could you describe your problem in more abstract terms?

- Who else, outside your own industry, deals with that type of problem?

- Who seems *not* to have this problem, even if they are in a similar situation? What are they doing differently?

Can we broadcast the problem widely?

Recall the DSM case and how the company found a solution by broadcasting its problem via a simple slide deck. If you can't identify someone who has solved the problem, could you do something similar?

chapter 7

look in the mirror

Can you teach reframing to small kids?

This question brought me to Hudson Lab School, a progressive, project-based school in Westchester, New York. The founders, Cate Han and Stacey Seltzer, knew of my work and challenged me to try running my reframing workshop with their students. So there I was on a warm August morning, teaching reframing to a fidgety bunch of five-to-nine-year-old kids.

The problems of little humans

You might be wondering what kind of problems kids that age have. Well, here's a choice selection from the workshop, lightly edited for inverted letters, fruit-juice accidents, and squiggly little hearts crowning all instances of the letter *i*:

> *"There was a rock I wanted, but it belonged to someone else."*

> *"I can't beat Electabuzz" (a video-game monster).*

> *"I can't hit my sister, because she is smaller than me."*

Yes, of such deep existential problems is the world of little humans composed. (In fairness, the one about wanting someone else's rock could be said to underlie pretty much every human conflict since the Peloponnesian War.) And as I ran the class with Stacey, Cate, and their colleagues, it became clear that most of the kids—especially the younger ones—struggled with the concept of reframing.

Take the case of a kid I'll call Mike, whose brother would sometimes hit him when they fought. Mike's problem statement was succinct:

I can never get revenge.

His chosen solution was similarly straightforward:

Hit on head first.

Based on my workshop, Mike realized that he might benefit from developing an alternative approach. After some hard thinking, he came up with:

Don't hit.

Despite Mike's valiant efforts, one sensed a certain systemic drift toward the first solution. I suspect Mike and his brother's conflicts continued to be solved through realpolitik rather than reasoning.

And yet, there were exceptions. Try for a second to step into the socks of Mike's classmate, a seven-year-old girl I'll call Isabella, and consider how she might reframe her problem:

My five-year-old sister, Sofia, constantly *asks me to come upstairs and watch television with her. This is very annoying.*

At first, Isabella leapt to the conclusion that the problem was her sister's personality: Sofia is an annoying person and thus, she naturally enjoys pestering her poor sister.

In doing so, Isabella illustrated what's called the fundamental attribution error, a noted phenomenon in psychology in which we instinctively conclude that people do bad things because they are, at heart, bad people. *My spouse is selfish. Our customers are stupid. People voting for the other side just want to see the world burn.*

It's an easy perspective to take—in fact, we do it automatically—and left to her own devices, that's probably what Isabella would have continued to think. But as she started questioning her problem, gently prodded by one of her teachers, she came up with two alternative framings:

Reframe #1: *How can I feel less annoyed with Sofia?*

Reframe #2: *How can Sofia be less lonely?*

In the first reframing, Isabella turned her attention to herself, exploring how she could manage her own emotions. In the second reframing, she stepped beyond the simplistic "she's just annoying" view and did something borderline remarkable: she started seeing her sister in a kinder, more human light.

In the next chapter, we'll take a closer look at how you can solve problems by taking someone else's perspective, deliberately working to truly understand them. Before that, we'll look at one of the most overlooked sources of insight: our own contribution to the problem.

Look in the mirror: What is my own role in creating this problem?

The strategies we've covered so far were all about seeing something that was hidden outside the frame—a bright spot, a higher-level goal, or a missing stakeholder.

This chapter, in contrast, is about a factor that tends to be hidden in plain sight right inside the frame—and that's *you*. When considering problems, we too often overlook our own role in the situation, as individuals or as a group.

Perhaps this is not surprising. Since childhood, we've learned to tell stories that conveniently leave out our own agency. Windows and vases break. Siblings spontaneously start crying. Milk-laden glasses, tired of their table-bound existence, fling themselves to the floor.

Research shows that this pattern continues unabated into adulthood. Examples of this abound. Here I'll mention a story that's 1) very possibly anecdotal and 2) too good not to share anyway. Reportedly, a 1977 newspaper article looked into what drivers wrote in their insurance-claim forms after they'd been in a car accident:

"A pedestrian hit me and went under my car."

"My car was legally parked as it backed into the other vehicle."

"As I reached an intersection, a hedge sprang up, obscuring my vision."

Whether anecdotal or not, the quotations capture something true: we're consistently pretty terrible at seeing ourselves clearly—and we reliably fail to take our own actions into account when faced with a problem.

Three tactics for looking in the mirror

The good news is, there are things we can do to get a more accurate perception of ourselves. Here are three tactics for better uncovering your own role in problems:

1. Explore your own contribution.

2. Scale the problem down to your level.

3. Get an outside view of yourself.

I should warn you, however, that this strategy can be more painful than the others. It's not too taxing to look outside the frame or rethink goals, and identifying bright spots can be positively delightful. But taking a long, hard look in the mirror, honestly confronting our own role in a problem, can be uncomfortable. Like a dentist's appointment, some people will go to great lengths to avoid it.

My advice: accept the discomfort. Our capacity to recognize painful truths can at times generate some of the most liberating solutions. In fact, some of the best problem solvers I've met don't just embrace or accept the pain of self-reflection. They actively seek it out, because they know that it carries the promise of progress.

1. EXPLORE YOUR OWN CONTRIBUTION

Have you ever used a dating app or a dating website? If you have, you might have noticed that people's written profiles change over time, reflecting their experiences with the app.

As people first create a profile, they write the usual happy inanities: *I like puppies, motorcycles, and long walks on the beach.* Soon after, though, details are added to their profile that tell you something about how their first couple of matches went:

- *Please write more than "What's up?" when you message me.*

- *Please look like your pictures.*

- *If you don't look like your pictures, you're buying me drinks until you do.*

Then there are the "no drama" people. These are the men and women who write on their dating profiles, "I'm not into drama"—or as they sometimes put it: "NO DRAMA!!!!!" When you see this on someone's profile—especially the CAPS LOCK version—you can surmise that they have experienced a good deal of drama in their past relationships.

Now, why might this be? Innocent explanations include that they've been unlucky, or that they happen to live in an area with lots of drama-prone people. But at the same time, one can't help but suspect a more tantalizing possibility: *they are the ones causing the drama,* or at least cocreating it.

Even if they aren't creating the drama, it's likely that they tend to *select for partners that create drama*—which should perhaps prompt a review of whatever filtering methods they use to pick their dates.

I share this example because our lives can sometimes provide similar clues about how our own behavior might play a role in creating the problem: *Nobody ever gives me honest feedback. Well, not since I fired that guy who whined all the time.*

When facing a problem, take the time to ask: *Is it possible that my (or our) own behavior is, on some level, contributing to the problem?*

- Headquarters/legal/compliance rejects almost every single idea we send them! *Should we rethink the way we develop or pitch our ideas?*

- Our salespeople are super sloppy. They make lots of errors in their reports, and they turn them in late. *Might our reporting forms be in need of simplification? Can we process them differently?*

- Our employees are not very good at collaborating with each other. *What are we, as leaders, doing to create that behavior?*

- I constantly have to tell my kids to put down their electronic devices. *Is it possible I was telling them this while checking something on my phone?*

Avoid the word *blame*

As you can probably sense, looking in the mirror can be challenging in practice. This goes double when a group is involved—because often, the problem was caused by someone in the room. (Or worse yet, the problem *is* someone sitting in the room.)

One helpful way to make the discussion easier is to avoid the word *blame*, and instead talk about the idea of "contribution." This advice comes from the management classic *Difficult Conversations*, coauthored by Douglas Stone, Bruce Patton, and Sheila Heen of the Harvard Negotiation Project. As Sheila told me:

Asking "who's to blame" can be problematic, because it really means, *Who messed up and should be punished?* The word *blame* suggests that someone did something that was objectively "wrong"—say, breaking a rule or acting irresponsibly. *Contribution* doesn't have that assumption: much of what you contributed might have been perfectly reasonable, but it still didn't help. Contribution is also a more forward-looking perspective, because it tells us what we would have to change to do better next time. And crucially, it recognizes that mistakes are typically the result of more than one person's actions. *Yes, you taking the wrong turn made us miss the flight. But in fairness, if I had booked a later departure, we would have had more room for error.*

Recognizing that several people contributed to a mistake, however, doesn't mean their contributions are evenly distributed. It still can be mostly one person's actions that created the result. The important part is to see the problem as a system, so you can identify all possible avenues of improvement instead of focusing on just one person's actions. As the inimitable Swedish statistician Hans Rosling put it: "Once we have decided who to punch in the face we stop looking for explanations elsewhere."

Here's how one leader from the oil and gas industry, John, practiced it back when he managed a factory:

> When something had gone wrong on the factory floor, the involved parties were called into my office to talk it over and figure out how we could do better. In that situation, people are naturally worried about being blamed, leading to some defensiveness—and that's really not a good way to prevent future problems. So I made a habit of always opening the conversation with a specific question: *Tell me how the company failed you.*

The question had a powerful effect on people, as they understood that the boss wasn't just looking for someone to blame. John's openness would prompt them to reciprocate by exploring their own contributions as well as those that were external, leading to a productive conversation about how to prevent the problem from recurring. By focusing on contribution rather than blame, and by being open to the possibility that mistakes have multiple parents, John and his employees jointly managed to create significant improvements at the factory.

2. SCALE THE PROBLEM DOWN TO YOUR LEVEL

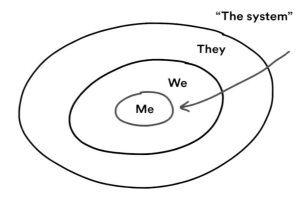

There is a deep temptation to frame problems at a level where you can't really do anything about them:

- *We can't innovate until the CEO decides to make it a real priority.*

- *Moving faster? Our corporate IT system would need a major overhaul before that could happen.*

- *I'll start writing my prize-winning novel the second I can afford a new laptop, some professional writing software, and a half-year sabbatical at a little lakeside cottage in Italy.*

The insistence on a systems-level problem framing can lead to "boil the ocean"–type efforts or paralysis through sheer fatalism. Author and columnist

David Brooks puts it like this: "To make a problem seem massively intractable is to inspire separation—building a wall between you and the problem—not a solution."

To counter this, remember that there are often things you can do at your own level even when the problem seems big. The critical tactic is to scale the problem down, asking, *Is there a part of the problem I can do something about? Can I solve the problem at a more local level?*

A "wicked" problem: corruption

Consider corruption. As you'll know if you've ever lived in a country plagued by corruption, this social pathology touches almost every aspect of society, including the cultural norms—*everyone is doing it, so why shouldn't I*—making it very hard to combat. Corruption has been called a "wicked" problem, which is not surfer-speak for a really awesome problem, but a term for challenges that are so complex as to be almost unsolvable.

And yet, people within a corrupt system sometimes find ways to fight back on their level. One inspiring case comes from Ukraine's health-care system. As described by the journalist Oliver Bullough, the supply chain for Ukraine's hospitals used to be a hotbed of corruption. Every time the hospitals needed to buy medicines or medical equipment, a number of corrupt middlemen siphoned off cash, resulting in vastly inflated prices and missing equipment. That

would be bad for any business. When that happens in a hospital, patients needlessly suffer and sometimes die.

The situation abruptly changed for the better when some civil servants in Ukraine's health ministry pushed through a policy change. How? They outsourced the purchasing of medicine to foreign agencies at the United Nations, thereby cutting out all of the corrupt middlemen in one stroke. The initiative, Bullough writes, saved hundreds of lives and led to $222 million in savings.

Ukraine still suffers from severe corruption issues. But in one small way, the problem was partially solved because bureaucrats, accountants, and health-care experts decided to see what they could do at their level, rather than accepting the status quo. In the same way, can you reframe the problem in a way that allows you to act on it?

3. GET AN OUTSIDE VIEW OF YOURSELF

In her book *Insight*, the organizational psychologist Tasha Eurich draws an important distinction between internal and external self-awareness.

- **Internal self-awareness** is when people are in touch with their own emotions. This is what people normally think of as "knowing yourself": being deeply attuned to your own values, goals, thoughts, and feelings.

- **External self-awareness**, in contrast, is your awareness of how *other* people see you. Do you understand the impact your behavior has on the people you engage with?

Eurich's point is that the two qualities aren't necessarily linked: someone can have spent the last six months on a mountaintop, serenely meditating on their core values and beliefs, and still be utterly clueless about the fact that everyone around them thinks they're arrogant and uncommunicative.* To solve people-related problems, try to become more aware of how you come across to others.

---

*At this point, some people go "I had a boss just like that!" In the spirit of this chapter: if that's you, maybe also consider if one of your subordinates ever felt the same way.

How to ask for input on yourself

My friend and fellow author, the social psychologist Heidi Grant, has a simple tip for how to do this. Find a good friend or colleague and ask that person: "When people first meet me, what impression do you think they get—and how do you think it differs from the way I really am?"

As Heidi says, "The questions will give you some immediate insight into sides of yourself that you may not have been aware of. And by asking them about a stranger's perceptions instead of their own, you open the door for people to share less positive opinions as well." (*Well, Bob, I think people might mistake your general mediocrity for extreme incompetence.*)

By the way, you may notice that this tactic is different from the other ones I've shared: it focuses less on the problem at hand and more on yourself. By improving your external self-awareness, you will gain an edge both with regard to your current problem and to all future problems you come across. (Consider this an added incentive for trying out Heidi's question.)

Overcoming power blindness

If getting honest feedback from your peers can be hard, getting it from people you lead can be even harder—and not just because the power imbalance may make them less likely to give you honest feedback. Columbia University psychologist Adam Galinsky and his colleagues have demonstrated that having power makes people less capable of understanding others' perspectives.

To remedy that and get a truly accurate perspective on a problem involving your employees, you may need to draw on outsiders. Here is an example from a company that did that.

Chris Dame reframes a usability problem

Remember Chris Dame, the designer who worked on Stephen Hawking's wheelchair? Some years ago, Chris was brought into a *Fortune* 500 company to help solve a problem. Specifically, the client had recently bought a software platform that allowed the company's employees to share knowledge and resources across different projects. The problem was, nobody actually used the system. As Chris told me:

> Based on their own conversations with their employees, the client came to us thinking they had a usability problem. People had told them things like, *It's too much of a hassle to put in the information. I simply don't have the time to get it done.* That framing of the problem suggested they had to simplify the system, which is more or less what we had been called in to do.

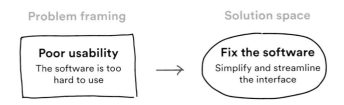

Problem framing   Solution space

Poor usability
The software is too hard to use

→

Fix the software
Simplify and streamline the interface

Chris, however, understood the importance of questioning that diagnosis:

> In my experience, when clients come to me with a problem, four out of five times, there is something about the problem that needs to be rethought. In maybe one of those four cases, the problem they are initially focused on solving is flat out the wrong problem.

For that reason, Chris started by setting up a series of small workshops in which he could explore the problem together with the employees, without the presence of the senior executives:

> Once they were free to talk to an outsider like me, off the record, a quite different problem came to the surface. Basically, people felt there was job security in hoarding information—and that sharing their knowledge and contacts put them at risk for being replaced, while not providing any career benefits.

Chris learned this wasn't just a perception. The company mainly rewarded and promoted people based on which projects they had been part of. As a result, everyone constantly hustled to get onto the winning projects, while having no incentive to help anyone else.

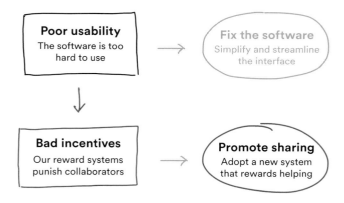

The insight led the client to change its incentive system. The company created a new metric, an "expert rating" that measured how many colleagues you had helped and how happy they were with your help. This expert rating was made visible to everyone else, creating a public way of acknowledging high-value contributors—and crucially, the management team also started using the expert ratings in their promotion decisions. Once the new solution was implemented, employees started using the knowledge-sharing platform to great effect.

A note on corporate self-awareness

While Tasha Eurich and Heidi Grant's observations pertain to individuals, they carry over quite well to the corporate level. Just like people, companies can have a strong corporate culture and explicitly defined values, and still remain clueless about how others—not least customers and prospective employees—actually see them.

Often, the image isn't flattering. Fairly or not (and I'd argue that it's often unfair), big institutions—especially for-profit companies, but also governmental organizations—are generally viewed in a negative light by the public. As my colleague Paddy Miller liked to put it: "When did you last see a Hollywood movie where a big corporation was cast as the good guys?"

For people working in large companies, facing this reality can be demoralizing. Employees of pharmaceutical companies, dedicating their careers to saving lives, are deeply troubled when they realize that some consumers see their corporations as being less trustworthy than tobacco companies. People who go into public service to do good are confronted with deeply jaded stereotypes about politicians and the public sector. Startups that grow big and successful may well continue to think of themselves as scrappy outsiders doing good work and fighting the ornery incumbents—all while their customers gradually shift to seeing them more like the incumbents.

In all of these cases, taking a hard look in the mirror is an essential step in making things better—even if it's a painful process to go through.

look in the mirror

Revisit your own problem statements. For each problem, do the following:

Explore your own contribution

Recall the idea of focusing on contribution rather than blame that Sheila Heen and her coauthors talk about. Problems can be the result of multiple people's actions, including yours.

- Ask yourself: What is my part in creating this problem?

- Even if you don't contribute to the problem, ask whether you can react differently to it (recall how seven-year-old Isabella did this with her younger sister).

Scale the problem down to your level

Problems can exist on many levels at once. Corruption, for instance, exists at a personal level, an organizational level, and a societal level. Not all problems are caused by your actions or at your level—but that doesn't mean that a problem can't be addressed at your level, at least in part. For problems that seem too big to solve, ask: Is there a way to frame the problem that makes it actionable at my level?

Get an outside view of yourself

Remember the concept of external self-awareness: How do you come across to other people? To map this more accurately:

- Ask a friend to assess how strangers might see you.

- If you are a leader—or if you are exploring a corporate-level problem—consider getting the help of neutral outsiders to gain an external view of the organization.

Finally, with all three tactics for looking in the mirror, be prepared for possibly unpleasant discoveries. Sometimes you need to go through a bit of pain to find the best way forward.

take their perspective

A CHALLENGE: DID THE POSTERS WORK?

When I visit office buildings, it's not just elevators that catch my eye. I'm also fascinated by *internal marketing posters*—that is, the posters people put up in hallways and meeting rooms to let their colleagues know about new in-house initiatives.

A tale of three projects

On the next page, you can see sketched examples of such posters, taken from three different *Fortune* 500 companies I've worked with. (The two on the bottom are from the same project.) In all three cases, an internal team was trying to get their colleagues to sign up for a new, web-based initiative.

Study the posters one by one. For each poster, first, guess whether it worked or not: Did people sign up for the service? Then articulate why. What is it about each poster that made you think either *Yes, that worked* or *No, people probably didn't sign up*? A quick hint: at least one succeeded, and at least one failed. You are given very little information, of course, so there's no shame in getting it wrong.

The answers to the poster challenge will be shared one by one as you read through this chapter.

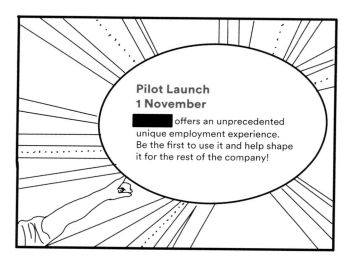

THE ART OF UNDERSTANDING EACH OTHER

I'm fascinated by posters like these, because they provide evidence of each team's ability to *understand the people they were trying to reach*. Discovering how others see the world—and in particular, how they see it differently from you—is perhaps the most fundamental form of reframing there is, and it is central to many of the challenges we face, at work, at home, and globally.

The bad news is, we're not terribly good at understanding other people's perspective on things. Like the movie *The Matrix*, it's as if we're running a simulation of other people inside our own heads—only the simulation is often crude and low-powered, getting us into all sorts of trouble as we make wrong guesses about what friends, customers, and colleagues really think and feel.

The good news is, our ability to understand others isn't a fixed, immutable trait. Research has shown that you can improve your understanding of others—and that doing so tends to lead to better outcomes. So, how do you do that?

One way, of course, is to go out and spend time with the people in question: if you want to know someone better, increasing your personal exposure to that person is not surprisingly a good (and research-backed) idea.

At the same time, exposure is not the whole answer. If regular exposure were enough, our bosses would understand us pretty well, and our partners and families would understand us perfectly. As family conflicts show, however, it's possible to spend a literal lifetime with someone and still not understand his or her perspective.

The strategy: take their perspective

This is where **perspective taking** comes into the picture. If exposure is the physical act of going out and investing time in getting to know someone, perspective taking is the cognitive equivalent: investing mental energy in thinking carefully about what it might be like to be in the other person's shoes, and what a given problem or situation might look like from that person's vantage point.

We normally call this "empathy," but perspective taking is more than that. In the research literature, *empathy* is normally defined as your ability to feel what someone else is feeling. Perspective taking, in comparison, is a broader, more cognitively complex phenomenon in which you aim to understand another person's context and worldview, not just his or her immediate emotions.

As an illustration of the difference, imagine that your neighbor is building a fence and hits his finger with the hammer. Empathy is feeling his pain when he hits his finger. Perspective taking is understanding why he thinks it necessary to build the fence. (You may also run into the term *sympathy*, which is to feel pity or compassion for him without necessarily feeling his pain.)

Perspective taking is not just a helpful supplement to exposure or other forms of real-world engagement (some of which we'll cover in the next chapter). It is often a *prerequisite* for it—because if you think you already understand people, why would you waste time talking to them? Sometimes, perspective taking may be the only viable option—because you may not always have the time, or even the opportunity, to go and get more exposure to people. (You certainly won't have that time during a ten-minute reframing discussion, unless someone was smart enough to invite the relevant people into the room.)

Here are three crucial steps to getting perspective taking right:

1. Make sure it happens.

2. Escape your own emotions.

3. Look for reasonable explanations.

1. MAKE SURE IT HAPPENS

When it comes to perspective taking, the most frequent mistake people make isn't that they do it poorly. It's that they *don't do it at all*. Nicholas Epley, a leading researcher in perspective taking, put it like this in a paper he coauthored with Eugene Caruso: "There is no more immediate barrier to accurate perspective taking than failing to use it in the first place."

Our failure to activate our other-people simulator has been found in lots of studies. In one memorable example, researchers Yechiel Klar and Eilath E. Giladi asked students to answer the question, *"How happy are you compared to the average student?"* But as they found, people didn't actually answer that question. Instead, the students seemed to answer the much simpler question, "How happy are you?" completely chopping off the part requiring them to think about how happy other students might be. Taking other people's perspective is an *active* behavior, like having to turn on a light switch.

Given this discussion, consider again the barometer poster shown here. Is there anything that strikes you about the communication choices?

I see two mistakes. One is subtle: the adoption barometer is set at around 30 percent. What this tells people is that *the majority of their colleagues haven't signed up for the initiative*. As detailed by the psychologist Robert Cialdini, among others, this type of negative social proof is likely to depress the sign-up rate.

The second mistake is more glaring: the message is all about the needs of the message *sender*. The team behind the poster was genuinely trying to help people. But from the poster they made, a casual observer might well conclude that the team cared only about themselves. "Help us reach *our* goal"? Imagine if companies did the same thing in their external advertising: *L'Oreal—Because We Want Your Money*.

Asking for help like this can work if people identify strongly with the sender, or if the goal is widely considered a capital-G Good Cause: *Help us reach our goal of zero traffic deaths*. Otherwise, you are better off framing your message around the receiver's needs.

The people behind the poster were talented, and ultimately their project did become successful, in part because of their dedication to building a good service. When they tried to communicate it, though, they unthinkingly defaulted to their own egocentric perspective rather than thinking about their audience. As a result, the adoption of their initiative went slower than they would have liked.

To avoid this trap, the first and most important step is simply to make sure perspective taking happens. Here's how:

- When you wrote down your problems in the Frame step, remember how I also asked you to list the stakeholders? For each stakeholder you identified—including those you may have added after looking outside the frame—make sure you invest active effort in understanding each of them.

- If you don't use the reframing canvas, make sure whatever process you use has a step that triggers perspective taking.

2. ESCAPE YOUR OWN EMOTIONS

Thinking deliberately about the stakeholders is just the first step. As described by the famous behavioral economists (and key reframing thinkers) Daniel Kahneman and Amos Tversky, effective perspective taking has two parts to it: *anchoring* and *adjustment*.

Anchoring is what happens once you switch on your other-people simulator. To figure out what they think and feel, you imagine yourself stepping into their shoes, and then you ask, "How would I feel if I were in their situation?"

Anchoring is better than nothing, but it has an evident flaw: not all people think like you. Imagine a senior leader who's preparing a speech: *If I were a frontline employee, how would I feel about the reorganization we're about to announce? Why, a bit hesitant maybe, but mostly I'd be really excited about the new opportunities it might bring!* After all, earlier in her career, the leader got her own first big chance because of a

reorganization—and she may never have been in a position where being laid off would be a catastrophic event for her.

That's where adjustment comes in. *Adjustment* means to adjust *away from your own preferences, experiences, and emotions*, asking "How might they see things differently from me?"

- If I were in my competitor's situation, I'd consider this a great deal. *But maybe they know something I don't.*

- If I lived in this district, my number-one priority would be to improve the local schools. *But maybe voters here have bigger problems on their minds.*

- If I were my best friends, I'd be *so* excited about the idea of flying to Paris for my bachelor party!

But okay, I know some of them are strapped for cash, so maybe they would prefer somewhere cheaper.

- Back when I was eight, I'd have played with this cool red fire truck for hours! *But maybe today's eight-year-olds are a bit more blasé about non-internet-enabled toys.*

People may anchor fairly well, but fail on the adjustment part. Studies have shown that if people are distracted or under time pressure, for instance, or if they are simply not aware of the need to adjust, they're more likely to arrive at the wrong conclusions. They are also less likely to remember that groups of people may react in different ways, rather than as one coherent entity.

The pilot launch poster

Now, consider again the pilot launch poster. What do you notice about the poster, given this discussion?

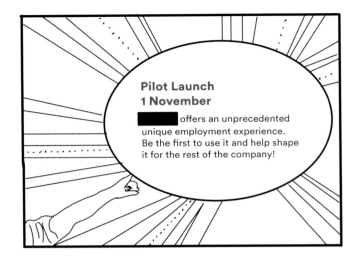

The poster was *not* successful at converting people. In fact, the entire project was eventually closed down for lack of use. And while the full story is more complicated than I can do justice to here, a key factor was the team's failure to comprehend that their colleagues did not see the project *in the same way as the project team.*

Consider the call to action: "Be the first to use it." Clearly, the team had devoted *some* effort to perspective taking by asking, "If I worked here, what might motivate me to sign up?" (That's the anchoring part.) Only, the answer they arrived at was, *Well, people like to be pioneers—that'll be a great selling point!*

That probably held true for the team members (who, after all, had pioneered a new project). But according to studies of how innovations spread, only 2.5 percent of people like to be guinea pigs for new things. All other people—twenty-four out of twenty-five—like to see that someone else has already tried them with a positive result, before joining in.

Also notice how the poster presents the initiative: "an unprecedented unique employment experience." Clearly the team felt excited about their project and its potential to bring about a totally new way of working. Their mistake was to assume that everyone else shared their enthusiasm. Not many people wake up in the morning and think, *What I'd really like right now is a hot cup of coffee and an unprecedented unique employment experience.* Most of us just try to get things done.

Incidentally, the fate of the project is also testament to the idea that exposure is not enough. It's one thing if someone in a faraway headquarters didn't truly understand his or her frontline employees in the field. But the project team worked *in the same office* as the people they tried—and failed—to recruit.

Good perspective taking requires genuine, focused, and deliberate effort. One helpful metaphor is the idea of an *emotional gravity well*. Just as a rocket needs energy to overcome earth's gravity and achieve orbit, you, too, have to expend energy to rise beyond your own emotions and viewpoints. If you don't, you'll remain helplessly trapped in your own perspective. To avoid that, try these three things:

Don't stop at the first right answer. When you try to guess what other people are thinking or to understand their motives, look beyond your first answer, *even if it feels true*. In their research, Nicholas Epley and colleagues found that "adjustments tend to be insufficient, in part, because people stop adjusting once a plausible estimate is reached." You get better results if you go beyond your first correct-sounding answer.

Examine people's context, not just their emotions. When trying to understand other people's perspective, don't just focus on their emotions. Consider as well what their context is, what they know and don't know, and other nonemotional aspects of their lives.

Explicitly ask people to step away from their own perspective. In a study of 480 experienced marketing managers, the researcher Johannes Hattula found that he could make them better at predicting what consumers wanted simply by reminding them to step away from their own perspective. Say something like: "Remember that people may feel differently than you do. Try to suppress your own preferences and focus only on understanding how they may think."

The pfizerWorks project

There is one more approach to perspective taking to discuss, but first, I want to contrast the first two projects with the third one—which, as you can surmise, was successful. The project was from Pfizer, and in fact you already heard part of the story in chapter 6, when we discussed Jordan Cohen and Seth Appel's work to find analysts that mastered Western communication norms. (As you may recall, pfizerWorks allowed Pfizer's many employees to outsource the boring parts of their work to remote analysts.)

In some ways, the odds were against pfizerWorks: the team was based in headquarters, far away from the field employees they targeted. And yet, the campaign was successful. The service eventually gained more than ten thousand users within Pfizer and was rated as the company's number-one most helpful service a few years after its creation.

So what made the difference? Here are four key elements of how the team got perspective taking right.

Exposure by proxy. Jordan Cohen, the project's founder, had the insight to recognize that as a headquarters person, he didn't fully understand what life was like for field employees. So he recruited Tania Carr-Waldron, an influential leader with twenty years' of experience working on the front lines of Pfizer. Tania's presence provided a way to get the user's perspective into the team. (Imagine the difference if the team with the "unprecedented unique employment experience" had done that.)

Anchor in the "felt problems" of their users. People don't care about your solution. They care about *their own problems*. Knowing that, the team's posters didn't lead with the wonderful features of the service. Instead, they described problems that employees recognized from their daily lives (and that pfizerWorks could help solve): *I have eighteen hours to get these documents ready.* That got people's attention far more effectively than anything else.

Use social proof. The team understood that most people want reassurances before they try new things. Here's Jordan:

> When we launched pfizerWorks in a new office, we didn't start with the posters. We started with getting one or two people from that office to try the service. If they liked it, we asked, "Would you be okay if we put up a poster with you on it, just here in the office?" Then, when people walked by, they could see that someone they already knew was using the service. We also asked them to sign the

posters, for an added personal touch. That was key in getting people to try it.

Different framings for different audiences. The message to the frontline employees was straightforward: _Use us and you won't have to prep this report on Sunday._ But Jordan also had to sell the project to his more senior colleagues in headquarters—and for that, he made sure to consider what their context was:

> I first considered selling the idea as a cost-saving initiative: after all, we had the potential to save the company several million dollars. But in a company like Pfizer, with revenues in the billions, nobody in headquarters would get much excited by that. What they really cared about was productivity—so the message that resonated with them was, _Our most talented and highly paid people waste too much time on low-value work. Imagine how much more productive they could be if we took some of that grunt work off their plates._

3. LOOK FOR REASONABLE EXPLANATIONS

My native city of Copenhagen used to have parking meters lining the streets at regular intervals. After parking your car, you'd trudge over to the nearest meter and feed it money, which would yield you a slip of paper. You'd then take the paper slip back to your car to be placed, like vampire-repelling garlic, in the front window of your car to ward off parking tickets.

On my street, Gothersgade, the meters were positioned on both sides of the street, facing each other pairwise:

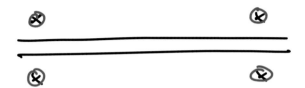

At first, the placement infused me with a touch of rage. Inevitably, the only free parking spot would be equally far from every meter, forcing me to trek arduously back and forth. _Typical clueless city planners!_ Couldn't they have figured out that it was much more efficient to stagger the placement of the meters so that people wouldn't have to walk as far?

In thinking that, I became a live example of the fundamental attribution error. When faced with an inconvenience, our first assumption is often that the people responsible for it are stupid, or uncaring, or even malicious. The effect is exacerbated when we don't know the people in question, but only have access to the systems they designed.

The truth is more complicated. Yes, sometimes people build systems without really paying attention to the needs of the end user. Yes, sometimes those people are not the sharpest knives in the drawer. And yes, you will also run into systems that were not designed with your best interests in mind, especially when commercial motives are involved. Just as often, though, there's a reasonable explanation behind the actions of other people: something that *you* might have done too, had you been in their shoes.

Take the parking meter placement. Having them face each other might have been optimal for technical or cost-related reasons, or perhaps to ease the work of the staff that collected money from the meters. But there was an even better reason, too, that was ultimately in my direct interest: they were placed that way *to prevent people from crossing the street.* (You may know the principle from those emergency telephones that used to dot the highways. They also faced each other pairwise, so that stranded motorists wouldn't start crossing the highway and risk getting run over.)

The benefits of a benevolent view

I share this story to highlight a key idea: when anchoring and adjustment fail to provide new perspectives, there's another method that might help—and that is to start from the assumption that people are trying to do good things (or at least, that they are not actively trying to pester you).

Ask questions like:

- Could this have an innocent explanation?

- Under what circumstances would I have done the same thing?

- What if they aren't stupid, careless, or evil? What if they are actually good people trying to do their best?

- Could their behavior actually be in my best interest?

- Might they at least think it is in my best interest because I haven't shared my real interests with them?

When an innocent explanation exists—perhaps the problem is caused by a third party or a simple misunderstanding—an overly punitive approach is evidently unfair, and research has shown that it risks starting a negative spiral of behavior.

Another category of explanation: people's behavior makes sense to them, even if it's problematic overall. Since it's hard to blame people for acting in their own interests—assuming they aren't being outright unethical—such problems are better reframed as systems problems rather than people problems.

Looking for such reasonable explanations doesn't necessarily mean that you should "forgive" the other party, or use the explanation as an excuse to let the problem continue. The situation may still be unacceptable, and people with good intentions may still be negligent in not realizing the actual impact of their actions.

But by explicitly searching for reasonable explanations and trying genuinely to understand other people's views, you'll have a better chance of resolving the situation positively. Even when you have to make people change their behavior, it often makes the conversation easier when you start by acknowledging their good intentions before discussing the actual impact of their actions. (*I realize you had good intentions when you handed our daughter a glue gun, but . . .*)

"It has to go viral"

For an example of how looking for reasonable explanations can help, consider the experience of Rosie Yakob, cofounder of the advertising agency Genius Steals.

Earlier in her career, when Rosie was leading the social media practice of the global advertising firm Saatchi & Saatchi, an internal client asked for help: the client wanted to engage with their fans on Facebook, and asked Rosie to put together a campaign for them. As Rosie told me:

> From the beginning, it was clear that the client didn't really understand how social media worked.

For instance, she was obsessed about the idea of having a YouTube video "go viral," something that understandably sounds exciting if you are an outsider. From our experience, however, we knew that actual user engagement—rather than just passive views—was a much better success metric, and so we designed a campaign that delivered on that.

The client, however, kept pushing for the viral video. So Rosie took the time to educate her on the nuances of social media:

> We gathered lots of case studies and examples, and set up a call with the client where we carefully explained why our approach was the right one. She understood everything and acknowledged that we were right—only to end the call by saying, "And you're gonna make the YouTube video go viral, right?" It was extremely awkward. We were tearing our hair out over this stupid client. She was asking us to do something that just didn't make sense.

After some thinking, though, Rosie started wondering. Apart from her ignorance of social media, the client didn't seem stupid. Was something else going on? To find out, Rosie invited the client out for drinks. And that's where the truth came out, two martinis in: the client's bonus was based on getting a million views on YouTube.

> Once we understood her situation, we changed tactics. What if we bought a million views—cheap, untargeted, essentially only so she'd get her bonus—

and then used the rest of the budget on things we knew actually mattered? She agreed to this, and then we finally got the go-ahead to do the campaign. It was not an ideal solution, but it was the best we could do given the situation—and the campaign delivered on the results.

———————

Compared with the subtleties offered by the other strategies, there is something surprisingly basic about perspective taking: *Remember to consider other people. Don't mistake your preferences for theirs. Oh, and con-sider if they are actually good people trying to do their best.* In my quiet moments, I say to myself: *We're pretty smart people, by and large. Do we really need to be told this kind of thing?*

Then I go poster spotting in the nearest large workplace—full of smart, talented people—and easily run across three bad posters for every good one. Until that ratio is flipped, I'll keep beating this drum. Next time you are in the office, take a look for yourself—and if you spot a particularly good (meaning bad) one, please send it my way. I'm starting a collection.

take their perspective

The strategy of taking their perspective is about deliberately investing time in understanding other people, thus avoiding wrong judgments about them and their actions. By getting into the habit of exploring a problem from the perspective of each stakeholder, you can get better at escaping the gravity well of your own worldview.

To do so, take the steps we discussed:

1. Make sure it happens

You'll get other people wrong unless you invest genuine effort in trying to understand them. Avoid this pitfall by using a stakeholder map:

- List each of the parties or people involved in the problem. Remember to look for hidden stakeholders, too, as we covered in the **look outside the frame** strategy.

- For each stakeholder, think about his or her needs, emotions, and general point of view. What are that person's problems? Goals? Beliefs? Context? What information do they have?

2. Escape your own emotions

When mapping the needs of the stakeholders, explicitly try to step away from your own perspective. If you do it with a group, remind your fellow group members that people may feel differently than they do themselves. Mention Johannes Hattula's research:

- "Research has shown that people focus too much on their own perspective when trying to understand others. Try to disregard your own preferences. Focus only on how they might feel and think."

By recruiting Tania Carr-Waldron to the pfizerWorks team, Jordan Cohen gained an invaluable resource who understood what people on Pfizer's front lines thought and felt. This helped Cohen's team build a useful service aimed at the right problems. If you don't have much exposure yourself, can you find someone like Tania who does?

3. Look for reasonable explanations

With the slow elevator problem, most people simply assume that the tenants are lazy or impatient. Fewer think about good reasons why they complain: might they be late for an important meeting?

In the same way, remember that most people consider themselves to be good, reasonable people. To avoid falling prey to negative stereotypes and cynical thinking, consider what reasonable explanations might cause the behaviors you see:

- Could there be an innocent explanation?

- Do the other people have valid reasons to act as they do—ones that aren't about stupidity or bad intentions?

- Is it possible that they are actually acting in my best interest—or that they at least think they are?

- Could this be a systems problem or an incentive problem, rather than a people problem?

move forward

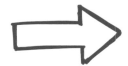

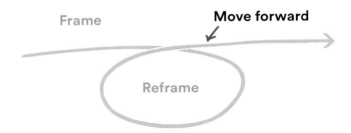

Kevin Rodriguez had a dream: he wanted to open a gelato store in New York, selling the delicious Italian ice cream he was such a fan of consuming.

As it happened, Kevin was a good friend of Ashley Albert, the entrepreneur behind the Royal Palms Shuffleboard Club. Naturally, he asked for her help in realizing his dream.

Ashley crushed Kevin's dream in less than eight hours.

She did this by inviting Kevin to walk around the city together, visiting gelato stores and chatting up their owners. As she told me:

> For the entire day, no matter where we went, we were never, ever in a situation where we couldn't find a nearby gelato store. And when we spoke to the owners, it became clear that it was not a very profitable business either: most of them survived by selling coffee. From the visits, one thing was totally clear: *this was not a problem that needed solving.*

At first glance, crushing someone's dream sounds like a bad thing. But consider the alternative: Kevin might have gone ahead and launched his gelato store, spending his savings and a few years of his life on something that would never take off. Ashley's insistence on a simple idea—*let's just go out and check how things are going for the gelato store owners*—allowed Kevin to shift his energy to a more promising problem (which he did; see the endnotes if you are curious).

Test your problem

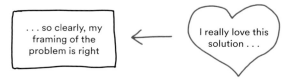

Most people know that you should test your solution before you commit to it. What is less well recognized is that before you test your solution, you should make sure to *test your problem*. Like a doctor who runs a few tests to confirm his diagnosis prior to operating, good problem solvers also work to confirm that they have framed the problem correctly before they switch back into solution mode.

This is a central point, because even the process of testing a solution can quickly become a serious time sink. In your excitement to build the solution, it's easy to think, *Hmm, what should I call my gelato store? Would a focus group help? What kind of ice should I sell? And how about the decor—can I get an interior designer to do a mock-up?* For technical solutions, the temptation is even greater: *Can we actually build this terribly exciting gadget I'm dreaming of? Let's head into the engineering lab for eight years and give it a try.*

What's worse, testing solutions can create a bad form of momentum that's unconnected to whether the problem is valid. Once you find the perfect name for your gelato store, it gets a lot harder to go back and challenge whether opening a gelato store is a good idea in the first place.

To avoid these situations, the last step in the reframing process is to *plan how you'll validate your problem framing through real-world testing.* Doing this closes the reframing loop (for now) and brings people back into solution mode. It is similar to action planning, but with the specific focus on making sure your efforts are pointed in the right direction.

In the following, I'll share four specific methods for problem validation:

1. Describe the problem to the stakeholders.

2. Get outsiders to help you.

3. Devise a hard test.

4. Consider "pretotyping" the solution

1. DESCRIBE THE PROBLEM TO THE STAKEHOLDERS

When he's dealing with armed hostage takers, the FBI hostage negotiator Chris Voss swears by a simple yet powerful technique called labeling. As Voss describes it:

> If you've got three fugitives trapped in an apartment on the twenty-seventh floor of a building in Harlem, they don't have to say a word for you to know that they're worried about two things: getting killed, and going to jail.

Voss doesn't start the conversation by trying to convince them to do anything: *you can't escape, so drop your weapons and come out or things will go badly!* Instead, he starts by labeling their fears, using a very specific wording:

> *It looks like* you don't want to come out. *It seems like* you worry that if you open the door, we'll come in with guns blazing. *It looks like* you don't want to go back to jail.

As Voss points out, there is something powerful about hearing your problem described accurately. Like you'll recall from the pfizerWorks posters—*these documents have to be done in eighteen hours?*—when someone shows that he or she understands your problem, it creates trust and opens the door to collaboration. Voss himself credits the method for resolving countless hostage situations. (And as he observes, if you get the problem wrong, you can always say "I'm not saying it's true. I just said it seems like that.")

Problem meetings

The method is useful not only to negotiators. If you need to validate your problem framing, one of the most cost-effective things you can try is simply to *describe the problem to the people that are involved.*

In the startup world, for instance, Stanford professor Steve Blank advocates for "problem meetings," in which you (as an entrepreneur) go to your intended customers and try to describe their own problems to them. The point is not to convince anyone of the framing, but to test whether it resonates. As Blank puts it, "Your goal is to get the *customers* to talk, not you."

Startup Cisco

I also saw the method used in a corporate setting, when Cisco employees Oseas Ramírez Assad, Edgardo Ceballos, and Andrew Africa created an in-house service called Startup Cisco that aimed at testing ideas rapidly.

"Cisco's people regularly come up with amazing ideas and technical innovations," Oseas noted, "but we weren't always great at testing those ideas quickly and seeing if they actually matched a problem our customers had. So we started running workshops that focused on doing that."

The need for rapid validation was inspired by an external consultant, Steve Liguori, who drew on his experience working with GE:

> There was a strong cultural norm of never showing anything to a customer until it was immaculate. Instead, the engineers would say, *We can build this,* and validation would typically happen in a room of executives saying, *How do we feel about this idea?* The customer would hear, *You're gonna love it,* for three years without actually seeing the thing. And then it would come out, and it would be perfect, but then the customer would say, *Okay, but*

why doesn't it do this? And then, when it didn't sell, people would go, *Oh, stupid marketing and sales people, they didn't sell it properly.*

In the beginning, a similar thing would happen at Startup Cisco's workshops. As Oseas said:

> People would come to us with strong ideas about the technical product they wanted to build, and would effectively reverse engineer the customer needs so they justified their idea. After trying that a few times, it became clear that we needed to delay the solution-building until the problem had been properly understood.

To gain that understanding, Oseas and his team relied heavily on the idea of connecting with clients early. Oseas commented on their method:

> We go to the client and say, "We are researching this issue. Is that issue actually a problem for you? Can you tell me more about that?" The key is to focus on their problem rather than the solution— because that's what makes them relate to it, and that's the core thing we need insights about. Are we getting their problems right?

In one instance, a Cisco veteran named Juan Cazila had come up with a promising idea for refineries and gas-extraction sites. However, the project had been stuck in Cisco's internal processes for about a year, so Cazila joined the Startup Cisco workshop to try to move it forward:

The team pushed me to ignore the usual processes and instead go directly to our customers and talk to them. So on day two of the workshop, we drafted an email and sent it to fifteen high-level executives at companies such as Exxon, Chevron and Shell.

That same afternoon, Cazila got on the line with three of the clients for an informal discussion. *We were wondering, do you have this problem at your refineries? You do? How much does that cost you?*

As it turned out, all three clients had the problem, and were very interested in solving it. Armed with this information, Cazila then contacted Cisco's head of services and requested resources to move the project forward. Two hours later, he got a positive reply, allowing the project to go ahead. As of this writing, the project has gotten funded and is being tested with one of Cisco's largest clients in Latin America.

2. GET OUTSIDERS TO HELP YOU

Outsiders can be a great resource to help validate your problems, as they're less emotionally attached to your preferred view of the problem (or solution). This can be particularly helpful when you aren't dealing with a product or service, but something less tangible.

For example, consider the experience of Georgina de Rocquigny, founder of the Hong Kong–based branding agency Untapped and an experienced hand at reframing.

One of Georgina's clients was a local management consulting company that had been around for a few years but had not yet defined a brand for itself. As the firm grew, it increasingly came up against other, more clearly branded competitors. That made the partners come to Georgina with a problem: *We need your help to brand ourselves as a strategy firm.*

The client's framing of the problem was understandable. In management consulting, there's an implied hierarchy between the strategic consulting houses and the more hands-on "implementation" firms. Strategic work is considered finer—and it often pays better too. For that reason, lots of consulting firms wish to be seen as strategy-focused.

Georgina, however, understood the need to validate the problem. So instead of starting in on the branding work, she convinced the client to let her interview some customers, employees, and partners. As she told me:

> The key thing was to get different perspectives into the process, to test whether they were solving the right problem. And as it turned out, they weren't. The client seemed to feel a mild sense of embarrassment about being at the more hands-on end of the spectrum: *We don't want to be perceived as just a body shop.* But as the interviews showed me, the clients actually liked that about them. Clients and collaborators alike said things like, *I hired them*

because they do more than strategy, and *I love working with them because while they are smart, they also aren't afraid of rolling up their sleeves and doing the work.*

Interview results in hand, Georgina convinced the consultants that they shouldn't try to brand themselves purely as a strategic partner, and should leverage—and be proud of—their ability to get things done. The end result was a powerful new positioning around bridging strategy and execution that has resonated with the firm and its clients, and has contributed to the firm's continued growth.

Georgina reflected on the process: "It's been interesting to me to see how big a role that feelings play in the job of defining yourself and your company's brand. Many clients come to me feeling slightly ashamed of what they do, thinking they need to become someone else to succeed. But often, when I talk to their clients, it turns out that the very thing that they are ashamed of is in fact a source of strength for them."

As Georgina's story shows, validating problems isn't necessarily a binary referendum on your problem, in which you discover either *Yes, I've got the right framing,* or *No, this framing doesn't hold water.* Sometimes your framing is correct overall—yet validating it surfaces an important nuance about the problem that leads to an even better solution. In this case, the consulting company was in fact right that it should aspire to a more strategic branding. Georgina's analysis didn't reject that idea. Rather, it helped the firm see that such branding wasn't incompatible with touting the company's execution-based strengths as well. The new positioning also differentiated the firm from the many others that tried to go for the strategy-only branding.

3. DEVISE A HARD TEST

When you are validating a problem, you are not just looking to find out whether it's real. It can be equally important to test whether the problem is big enough for your stakeholders to really want to solve it. The key to doing so is to devise a test that gets real answers out of the stakeholders. Here's a story of two entrepreneurs who did that.

How Managed by Q validated its problem

When Saman Rahmanian bought his first apartment, he decided to join the board of the building it was in. He quickly learned how much of a hassle it was to run a residential building:

> I was getting really frustrated by the cleaning provider in particular. They were reputed to be one of the better ones, but the service felt horrible. There was little transparency around whether they did their job properly—my wife would ask, "did they clean the stairs today?" and I wouldn't know. There were no good ways to communicate with the clean-

ing crew either, short of either calling their office or hoping that a Post-it note would be noticed and followed.

Saman got an idea: he could create a one-stop-shop service for residential buildings that would professionalize the delivery of cleaning and other services, so board members like him could manage their buildings with a lot less hassle.

Excited by the opportunity, Saman started exploring the idea with colleagues. One was the former community organizer Dan Teran, who ended up as Saman's cofounder.

Being well versed in lean startup practices, Dan and Saman set out, before they built the service, to validate that their idea was actually something customers cared about. To do so, they created a pitch deck describing the service as if it already existed, and then tried to sell it.

Saman explained: "We set up meetings with twenty different boards of residential buildings and spent a week visiting them and pitching the service. The reactions were very positive: many of them expressed interest and said it was a great idea."

If Dan and Saman had left it at that, they could easily have believed that they were right on track, and might have started building the service. But they knew from experience that that test was too easy: what customers say isn't necessarily the same as what they do. So, at the end of their pitch, they requested a down payment. *Great that you love our service! We have some open spots starting in a few months—so if you give us your credit card right now and make the first payment, you can secure a spot.*

As Saman explained: "Everything you are told before asking for people's credit card info is not to be trusted, no matter how positive they are. When you ask for their credit card details, *then* the real reservations come out."

Their caution was warranted. Only one of the twenty boards they pitched signed up for the service. Bad cleaning was indeed a problem—but clearly, not one that was big or urgent enough to prompt clients to take action.

That, however, was not the end of the story. During their tests, they met with a large commercial real-estate broker whose reaction was immediate: "This would be great in offices." Saman:

> We had a feeling that offices might work, and decided to tweak the sales pitch a bit and give it a try. So something like two weeks after our disappointing meetings with the residential boards, we set up twenty-five pitches to office managers. As it turned out, eighteen of them signed up with their credit cards after the first meeting. At that moment, we knew we had found the right problem to solve.

They named it Managed by Q—as a reference to the handy quartermaster in the James Bond movies. They would eventually go on to attract more than $100 million in funding and serve offices all over the country. They also gained acclaim for their innovative and humane labor practices. Breaking with the much-maligned contractor model employed by other start-ups, the founders decided to employ their cleaners full time, give them 5 percent of the company, and create real career paths for them. As a result, perhaps for the first time in history, cleaning has become more than a dead-end job.

Four years in, Dan—who had become the company's CEO—received a US government award on behalf of the company in recognition of its leading-edge labor practices. (Saman is off building his next startup, in the health-care space.) Shortly before this book went to press, Managed by Q was acquired for a sum reported to be over $200 million.

4. CONSIDER "PRETOTYPING" THE SOLUTION

In some cases, instead of validating the problem, it's possible simply to test the problem and the solution at the same time. The key is a method called "pretotyping." Coined by the Google employee Alberto Savoia, pretotyping is different from prototyping in that you don't actually build the solution at all, but instead focus on finding ways to simulate the product and see if clients will buy it.

Here's an example of that. Remember Henrik Werdelin of BarkBox and the Net-90 story? One day, at a team dinner, some of BarkBox's people started pitching new business ideas to each other for fun.

Inspired by an opened wine bottle, one partner said, *You know, I bet we could come up with a fun new dog-inspired design for wine stoppers.* Here's Henrik:

> One thing led to another, and suddenly, people got competitive. Somebody pulled out a laptop and drew a realistic 3-D model of a fun-looking wine stopper. Someone else thought, *Hey, I'm just going to set up a site where you can buy it.* A third person created an ad for the product and started running a few campaigns on social media. At no point during all this did anyone ever intend to actually pursue the idea.

The team sold their first wine stopper shortly after dessert was served, to a customer who saw it on Facebook. Henrik happened to have taken note of the time from idea to first real-world sale: seventy-three minutes.

Satisfied with having demonstrated their business prowess and fearing that their newly created monster would actually come to life and suck them into a branding Venn diagram involving dogs and alcohol, the team promptly closed down the site and refunded the customer's money.

Validating your problem is not *always* necessary. If you can test your ideas this quickly and simply, don't worry too much about problem diagnosis. Just throw stuff at the wall—or in this case the internet—and see what sticks.

————————

Once you've made a plan for how to move forward, the reframing process is at an end. However, one more step remains: to plan your next reframing check-in. To that end, we'll take a look at another domain in which regular problem check-ins are a matter of life and death.

THE IMPORTANCE OF REVISITING THE PROBLEM

When Scott McGuire arrives at the scene of an accident and finds someone who's hurt, he follows a simple routine called ABC:

Airway: Is the person's airway clear?

Breath: Is the person breathing normally?

Circulation: Is the person's pulse steady?

The test ensures that the patient is not in immediate danger before Scott starts treating them for other injuries. If Scott is alone on the scene, he does something else before starting treatment: he sticks a strip of tape on his leg and writes down the time for the next ABC check. "If the patient is in critical condition, I might check his vitals every three-to-five minutes. If he's more stable, I check every ten minutes. Writing it down is a way to make sure it gets done even if lots of other things are going on."

Since volunteering for a search and rescue team at age thirteen, Scott has served as a firefighter, an emergency medical technician, a wilderness guide, a mountain guide, and much more. In all these jobs, emergency protocols teach him to reassess the situation regularly:

> It can seem like backtracking, but it often reveals newly discoverable information. Sometimes the information was always present—but it requires a revisit of the original perspective to see it clearly. Other times, the situation changes. If someone has broken their ribs, they might not actually feel any pain the first time you check, because their adrenaline is acting like a painkiller. When you check their torso again ten minutes later, that's when you discover the problem.

Problem framing is similar to ABC checks in that you don't just assess the problem once—you have to do it at regular intervals.

In part, this is important because problems *change over time*. Even if your problem diagnosis is initially right, it's dangerous to stick with it, just as it would be dangerous for Scott to do only one ABC check and then assume everything was fine from

then on. As the design scholar Kees Dorst writes of organizations:

> [I]n conventional problem-solving, the "definition of the problem" is always the first step . . . but by defining the problem, they inadvertently freeze the context too, and more often than not this is a grave mistake that will come back to haunt them as they try to implement their new solution.

Regular check-ins also help in situations with time constraints. Instead of trying to complete the diagnosis upfront, it's generally better to do a swift round of reframing, move forward, and then return to the problem diagnosis again later, once you've gained more information.

FOUR WAYS TO REVISIT YOUR DIAGNOSIS

To make sure you revisit the problem on occasion, you can:

1. **Schedule reframing after each round.** At the end of a reframing process, immediately slot the next round into your calendar. The interval depends on the "clock speed" of your project, of course, but it's generally better to be overaggressive with scheduled check-ins.

2. **Assign the reframing role to someone.** When fighting fires, one of the people on Scott's team is assigned the role of incident commander. That

person's job is to stay at the back and monitor how the fire develops. In a similar manner, it can help to assign someone the job of keeping an eye on the problem and scheduling follow-ups.

3. **Create routines in your team.** Routine check-ins can be helpful. In disaster zones, Scott and his fellow emergency workers have a routine in which they have an all-hands meeting every four hours. The meeting might be as short as fifteen minutes. Similarly, teams that work with so-called agile methods often start every day with a "stand-up" in which each team member shares the problems he or she is working on. Can you incorporate reframing into some of your existing routines, such as in weekly staff meetings?

4. **Practice the mindset.** Finally, with enough practice, reframing will become second nature to people, allowing them to have a kind of "double vision" to keep both the solution and the problem in mind. In rapidly changing situations, this instinct can help trigger a new review of the problem, even in the absence of structural reminders.

move forward

Take a look at your problem statements. For each one, figure out how to move forward.

How can you test your problem?

Novice problem solvers look to confirm their theory: *Isn't my solution great? Let's see if we can do it.* Expert problem solvers don't try to confirm the framing they believe in—they look for ways to prove it wrong. Like Ashley did when Kevin pitched his gelato idea, is there a way to quickly engage with the real world to determine whether you are targeting the right problem?

To validate your framing of the problem, use one of the four tactics we covered:

- **Describe the problem to the stakeholders.** Like the Cisco team did, talk to the involved parties and describe the problem to them. Don't try to sell them on your framing. As Steve Blank points out, the idea is to see if your framing resonates and to get them to give you more information.

- **Get outsiders to help you.** If you suspect you are too close to your own idea—or if you think people won't give you honest feedback—can you use an outsider to help you? Remember Georgina's story about the consulting firm that used her to validate their assumptions around branding.

- **Devise a hard test.** Recall how Managed by Q used a credit card sign-up to test whether people really felt strongly enough about the problem they had in mind. How can you set up a similar test for your problem (or your solution)?

- **Consider "pretotyping" the solution.** If it's easy and risk-free to test a given solution, just go ahead and try it. Consider using Alberto Savoia's concept of pretotyping to find nimble ways of testing your solution, like the BarkBox team did with their wine stopper idea.

These are not the only ways you can validate a problem. If you need more inspiration, consult the startup literature—or better yet, talk to someone who has startup experience, just like Kevin did with Ashley.

Finally, before you close the reframing loop and swing back into action, make sure you have planned your next reframing check-in.

overcome resistance

three tactical challenges

COMPLICATIONS AND HOW TO HANDLE THEM

You now know everything you need to get started with reframing. There's more to learn if you want to achieve full mastery of the method, but much of that learning will come from practical experience as you apply it to your own problems and those of your clients, colleagues, and friends.

I still have more to offer, though. As you work on real-world problems, you'll eventually run into what I think of as *complications*. These are the various practical obstacles to reframing, such as when other people resist the process, or if you have no clue what's causing a given problem.

That's the topic of this part of the book. In the next chapter, I'll share advice on how to overcome resistance to reframing. In this chapter, we'll take a look at how to handle three common tactical challenges:

1. Choosing which frame to focus on (when you end up with too many framings)

2. Identifying unknown causes of a problem (when you don't have any idea what's going on)

3. Overcoming silo thinking (when people resist outside involvement)

This part of the book is meant as a go-to resource, so if you are eager to get started, just bookmark it and skip ahead to the final chapter, "A Word in Parting."

1. CHOOSING WHICH FRAME TO FOCUS ON

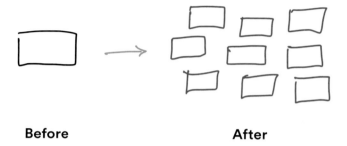

Before   **After**

When trying reframing for the first time, some people will likely voice a specific frustration: *When I started this, I had one problem. Now I have ten problems. Thanks, reframing method, veeery helpful.*

Feeling frustrated isn't necessarily a bad thing; it's a normal part of the process. At first it might be annoying that you no longer have a "simple" view of the problem—but generally, that's balanced out by the benefits of not solving the wrong problem.

Still, there is a very practical question to deal with: If you come up with multiple different framings of the problem, how do you decide which frames to explore and which to ignore?

In some situations, with very important, do-or-die problems, it makes sense to go through a methodical analysis of every single framing, reality-testing them one by one. Typically, though, you'll have neither the time nor the resources—nor the patience—to do that. Instead, you'll have to select one or two framings to focus on, at least until the next iteration of the process. How, then, can you best do that?

While problems are too varied for a fixed formula to work consistently, I've found three rules of thumb that can help. As you review the framings, pay special attention to the ones that are:

- Surprising

- Simple

- Significant-if-true

Explore surprising framings

When you reframe a problem, you (or the people you help) will sometimes express surprise at a specific framing: *Oh? I hadn't thought about that angle.* In my workshops, people have described it as an almost physical sensation—a visceral sense of relief upon finding a new perspective on their problem.

The sensation of surprise doesn't ensure the framing in question will ultimately be viable. Still, such framings should usually be explored. The feeling of surprise arises exactly because the framing breaks with a mental model that the problem owner has been trapped in—increasing the chances that the new perspective will help.

Look for simple framings

In the popular imagination, breakthrough solutions are often associated with complex new technology. The location function on smartphones, for instance, relies on quantum mechanics, atomic clocks, and orbiting satellites to accurately pinpoint where you are. Given that, it can be tempting to think the best solutions come from esoteric, highly nuanced approaches to the problem.

In my experience, that's rarely the case. In daily life, good solutions (and the corresponding problem framings) are fairly simple. Remember Lori Weise's solution to the shelter-dog problem, for instance. That was just about keeping the dogs with their first family. The best solutions often have a ring of retrospective inevitability. Once identified, people react with, *Of course! Why on earth didn't we think of that earlier?*

When you consider which reframings to pursue, you should generally gravitate toward the simpler ones. The medieval friar-philosopher William of Ockham is credited with the notion of "Occam's razor," which is a catchy way for scientists to say that when you face multiple possible explanations for a phenomenon, go with the one that's most straightforward.

Translated to workplace problems, take the following two framings and consider which one Occam's razor would point to: *People aren't buying our product because . . .*

We still haven't found the exact right marketing message despite cycling through four ad agencies VS Our product sucks

The emphasis on simplicity is a guideline, not an iron law. Some problems ultimately do require complex, multipronged solutions to be effectively resolved. But as Steve de Shazer wrote, in regard to his experience with therapy: "No matter how awful and how complex the situation, a small change in one person's behavior can make profound and far-reaching differences in the behavior of all persons involved."

Look for significant-if-true framings

Finally, it can sometimes make sense to test framings that you do *not* believe in.

Reframing, by nature, is about challenging your assumptions and beliefs about a problem. Sometimes, simply hearing a new, unexpected perspective can be enough to make you reconsider your previously held beliefs. But more often, when you come across a truly powerful framing, your gut reaction—or what we more nobly call our intuition—may well be negative. And when it comes to reframing, *you have to be careful about trusting your intuition.*

This may strike you as odd. After all, much of the personal advice industry lives on one message: trust your gut. We tend to trust our immediate feelings about something without really questioning where those feelings come from. But your "gut" is really just your brain's subconscious summary of what has worked in the past. And here's the thing: creativity often involves transcending your past experience, breaking with at least one or two of your assumptions. Your intuition is built from your past. For exactly that reason, it's not always a good guide to your future.

What that means is, even if a framing goes against your gut, you shouldn't dismiss it before asking: *If it were true, would this framing have a big impact?* Such framings can be worth exploring even if you think their odds of being right are minimal—provided the testing of that frame doesn't require excessive resources.

The Bolsa Familia program. One example comes from Brazilian politician and former president Lula da Silva. Most recently, Lula gained a level of infamy as he was found guilty of corruption. Before that, however, he attracted positive international attention by creating a successful initiative for alleviating poverty, the Bolsa Familia program.

As described in Jonathan Tepperman's book *The Fix*, the program shifted from trying to provide services to poor families to just giving the poor money, allowing the families to spend it on the goods and services they wanted.

Despite being simpler and cheaper—one study estimated it to be 30 percent less costly than providing traditional services—the idea of giving people money had been firmly rejected by local and international experts, most of whom were convinced that poor people would waste the money on vices and other frivolous things. Lula, however, had grown up poor, and knew that those prejudices were inaccurate: poor people—especially mothers—generally will spend money wisely. As a result of the Bolsa Familia program and other initiatives, Brazil's extreme poverty rate was cut in half, lifting thirty-six million people out of the most severe category of poverty and providing a bright spot for other nations' efforts to tackle income inequality.

The question that strikes me is, could one of those former policy makers have come up with the idea, *despite their instincts?* Using this test, they may have said, "I don't believe poor people can handle money responsibly. But I recognize that there's a small chance I am wrong about that assumption—and if I am, we could make a huge difference, because money transfers would be vastly more efficient than providing goods and services. With that in mind, why don't we set up a small experiment to test whether I'm right?"

Try to explore more than one framing

No matter which selection strategy you use, note that the point of this selection process isn't to arrive at one final framing. Some of the teams I've worked with picked a primary frame to explore, and then designated some of the team members to explore second or third frames as well. Unless you have to commit to an immediate solution, parallel explorations can be worth the effort. Failed avenues of inquiry will sometimes prove helpful later, even if it's just to tell a stakeholder, "We tested that angle, and it didn't work."

2. IDENTIFYING UNKNOWN CAUSES OF A PROBLEM

Imagine you face a problem, only your initial analysis (including your attempts to reframe it) didn't yield a clue as to what's causing it. What then?

We've already covered one method you can try, namely the idea of *broadcasting the problem*, which you read about in chapter 6, "Examine Bright Spots." Here, I'll share two other methods you can use to uncover the hidden causes of a problem: discovery-oriented conversations and learning experiments.

Discovery-oriented conversations

Sometimes, a simple conversation with the right person can be enough—provided you pay attention to what the person is really saying.

A few years ago, two entrepreneurs by the names of Mark Ramadan and Scott Norton launched Sir Kensington's, a line of condiments including ketchup, mustard, and mayonnaise. The idea was to create a tastier, healthier, all-natural alternative to the existing offerings.

Two years in, their products were selling well, and demand was growing. But for some reason, the sales of their ketchup lagged. The problem was not about the taste: customers said they loved it. But they were buying less of it than their enthusiasm suggested they would.

Mark and Scott thought it might be related to the shape of the bottle. When they launched the company, they had chosen to use square glass jars for all of their products to create a high-end brand: instead of a plastic squeeze bottle, people got a stout glass jar reminiscent of fancy mustards. The strategy served them well overall, judging by the sales of their other products. But it wasn't working with their ketchup.

Mark and Scott debated whether they should switch to a more traditional bottle shape, just for the ketchup. It was a big decision. Changing would affect every part of their supply chain and create complexity in operations. If they got it wrong, it would take a year to reverse the decision. Mark and Scott wanted to make sure they were doing the right thing—and that meant figuring out what was really going on with the ketchup sales.

Pause and consider what a big company might have done here. The head of marketing might have decided to run a survey, or bring together some focus groups. Or perhaps, the company would have forked over a couple of hundred thousand dollars to run an in-depth ethnographic study, having professional researchers follow people on their shopping trips and in their homes.

These methods would likely yield useful insights, and many big companies have used them to create growth. Being part of a startup, though, Mark and Scott didn't have the option of doing any of those things—so instead, they just started talking to people they knew: customers, investors, and friends who used their products. The clue came when one of their investors told

them: "I tried the sample you sent me, and I really love it. I still have it in my fridge."

That remark made Mark and Scott pause. The investor had received the bottle months earlier—so if he loved it, *why did he still have the original bottle in the fridge?* Why hadn't he used it up by now?

The answer turned out to hinge on a small detail about how most people store ketchup. Mark found that people tend to stock mustard and mayo on the main shelves, which leaves those condiments in plain sight the next time people open the fridge. Ketchup tends to get stuck in the shelves on the door. If the shelf's guardrail is transparent, that's not a problem. But in fridges with nontransparent guardrails, Sir Kensington's square ketchup bottle disappeared from view. As Mark put it, "If you can't see the bottle, you don't take it out as often. Out of sight, out of mind."

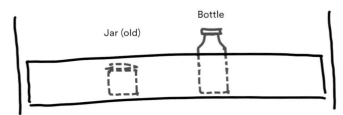

The discovery of the fridge problem gave Mark and Scott the confidence to change to a taller bottle. Once it hit the market, sales velocity increased 50 percent.

As the story shows, you'll sometimes find important clues in simple conversations—provided you pay attention to what's being said. When their investor casually mentioned that he still had the original bottle, other people might not have caught the significance of the remark. Mark and Scott, however, were attuned to it: they were listening for clues to the problem, which yielded the key piece of information.

What does it take to do this? The topic of listening and questioning has been widely explored within management science and elsewhere. A full summary is beyond the scope of this book, but I've listed three pieces of advice here on which there's widespread agreement.*

Step into a learning mindset (aka, shut up and listen). The management scholar Edgar Schein has pointed out in his work on "humble inquiry" that we too often start conversations with the aim of telling. A key step happens *before* you enter the conversation, as you remind yourself to approach the other person with an intent to listen and learn.

As an aside, when reframing problems in a group, try to notice your own talking-to-listening ratio. Given five minutes to discuss their own problem, some people spend four of the five minutes talking, leaving little room for input. If you tend to talk a lot as well, you might consider experimenting with listening more.

---

*If you feel you'd benefit from more advice on how to become a better listener, I have provided some recommendations in the appendix, under "Questioning."

Create a safe space. As shown by Amy Edmondson's work on psychological safety, learning conversations are less effective if people fear recrimination or otherwise feel they can't speak freely. Find ways to de-risk the conversation—or consider having a third party do the interviews.

Seek out discomfort. As we discussed in chapter 7, "Look in the Mirror," to get to the useful insights, you must be prepared to discover potentially painful truths about yourself. As MIT professor Hal Gregersen and his colleagues have documented, many leading business people credit their success in part to their ability to put themselves in uncomfortable situations. (This also applies to your selection of who you speak to: Do you seek feedback only from people who will tell you pleasing things?)

Run a learning experiment

If conversations don't yield any clues to the nature of the problem, another strategy might involve running a small *learning experiment*. A learning experiment, simply put, is a deliberate attempt to do things differently from how you normally do them, in order to shake things up and learn something new.

Jeremiah "Miah" Zinn did this when he worked at the popular children's-entertainment television channel Nickelodeon—home to immortal cultural figurehead SpongeBob SquarePants. Miah ran the product development team, which had just come up with an exciting new app aimed at kids aged seven to twelve. The team knew from testing that kids loved the content—and indeed lots of kids downloaded the app. But then, a problem appeared. As Miah put it: "To use the app, you had to go through a one-time sign-up process—and as part of that, you had to log into the household's cable TV service. At that point, almost every single kid dropped out of the process."

There was no way around the sign-up requirement, so Miah's team had to figure out how to guide kids through the process and increase the sign-up rate. And they had to do it fast: every day without a solution cost them users. Under pressure, they went straight to a method they knew exactly how to wield: usability testing.

"We set up hundreds of A/B tests," Miah said, "trying different sign-up flows and testing new ways of wording the instructions. Let's try twelve-year-olds in the Midwest—do they react better if we switch the steps around?"

There were good reasons for the team's reliance on A/B testing. Since its humble beginnings in the late 1980s, with the publication of Donald A. Norman's classic book *The Design of Everyday Things* marking the breakout moment, usability testing has become a common and powerful tool for tech companies. One big tech company famously tested more than forty shades of blue to find the exact right color for its search page.

But as Miah said, "The problem was, none of our tests moved the needle. Even the best ones only nudged the sign-up rate a few percentage points at most."

To break out of their rut, Miah decided to try something new:

> We had focused on gathering lots of data, looking at big groups. How many percent swiped here or tapped there? And that had gotten us nowhere. So I had a thought: Instead of studying lots of kids from afar, why don't we invite a couple of them into our office, parents in tow, and sit next to them and see what happens as they try to log in?

It was a pivotal decision. As Miah's team interacted with the kids, it became clear the problem wasn't about usability. The kids had no problem understanding the instructions or navigating the log-on process. (These days, most ten-year-olds can crack a safe in five minutes flat.) The problem was about their *emotions*: the request for the family's cable-TV password made the kids fear getting in trouble. To a ten-year-old, a password request signals forbidden territory.

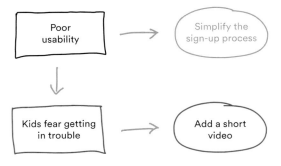

Miah's team immediately abandoned their efforts to fix the sign-up process. Instead, they produced a short video explaining to kids that it was perfectly okay to ask their parents for the password. *No worries, young grasshopper! You won't get in trouble by asking!* The result: an immediate tenfold increase in the sign-up rate for the app. From that day onward, Miah made sure that their product-development processes also included some in-person user testing in addition to their A/B testing.

Tests versus learning experiments. Miah's story shows the difference between testing and experimenting. When Miah's team first attacked the problem, they didn't stick only to analysis. They tested hundreds of different permutations of sign-up flows on real customers, in real time. If you had walked into their office and proclaimed, "Folks, we need to do some experiments to figure out the answer," they would have looked at you weirdly: *That's what we're doing!*

The issue was that their tests were focused on the wrong problem. The team found a way to move forward only with Miah's decision to try something different. Instead of continuing to tweak the usability testing—*What if we make the button sliiiightly more blue?*—Miah stepped back and asked, *Is there something else we can do to learn more about the problem? Something we haven't tried before?*

That is the essence of learning experiments: When you are stuck, instead of persisting with your current patterns of behavior, can you come up with some kind of experiment to help you cast new light on the situation?

3. OVERCOMING SILO THINKING

Most people agree that silo thinking is bad—and the research on innovation and problem solving backs that up. For complex problems, teams that are diverse outperform teams whose members are more similar to each other. With reframing in particular, getting an outsider's perspective on your problem is a powerful shortcut to identifying new framings.

In practice, though, people involve outsiders far less than they should. They may agree with the idea in theory, but when it comes to doing it, they say things like:

- *Outsiders don't understand our business, so it takes ages to explain the issue. We don't have time for that.*

- *I'm a leading expert in my field. What's the point of involving nonexperts?*

- *I've tried asking outsiders, and it didn't work. The ideas they came up with were useless.*

The reactions reveal something important: there are good and bad ways to involve outsiders. To get it right, consider the following story of a leader we'll call Marc Granger.

Soon after taking over a small European company, Granger realized he had a problem:

Our people aren't innovating.

To address this, the management team found an innovation training program that they believed would help. However, as they discussed how to roll out the training program, they got interrupted by Marc's personal assistant, Charlotte.

"I've been working here for twelve years," Charlotte said, "and in that time I have seen three different management teams try to roll out some new innovation framework. None of them worked. I don't think people would react well to the introduction of another set of buzzwords."

Charlotte's presence in the meeting wasn't accidental. Marc had invited her himself. "I had only taken over the company about half a year earlier," he said, "and I knew Charlotte had a good understanding of what was going on in the company. She was the kind of person that our employees came to when they had a problem they didn't want to take to management directly. I felt she might help us see beyond our own perspective."

That's exactly what happened. It quickly became clear to the team that they had fallen in love with a solution—the training program—before they had really understood the problem. Once they started asking questions, they discovered that their initial diagnosis was wrong. Marc: "Many of our employees already knew how to innovate—but they didn't feel very engaged in the company, and so they were unlikely to take initiatives beyond what their job descriptions mandated." What the managers had first framed as a skill-set problem was better approached as a motivation problem.

Marc's team dropped the training program and instead rolled out a series of changes aimed at promoting engagement: things like flexible working hours,

increased transparency, and active participation in the leadership's decision-making process. "To get our people to care about us," Marc said, "we first needed to demonstrate that we cared about them and were willing to trust them."

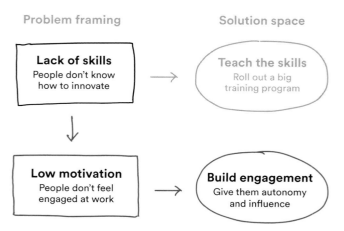

Within eighteen months, workplace-satisfaction scores doubled, and employee turnover—a big cost driver for the company—had fallen dramatically. Financial results improved markedly as people started to invest more energy in their work and took more initiatives. Four years later, the company won an award for being the country's best place to work.

If Marc hadn't invited Charlotte into the room, it's easy to imagine that the management team would have rolled out the training program and suffered the same fate as the three prior management teams. What was it about the process that worked, compared with the many times people struggle to make good use of outsiders? In part it was the *type of outsider* Marc brought in.

Look for boundary spanners

Charlotte's existing connection to the team was crucial, and runs counter to conventional wisdom about the power of outsiders. Published success stories on the topic often focus on how tough problems got solved by someone who was utterly unconnected to the issue: *None of the nuclear physicists could solve the problem! But then a balloon-animal artist came by.*

Stories like those are memorable, and the lesson they offer is backed by research. But as a consequence of hearing such stories, people often think that they have to seek out "extreme outsiders" who are *very* different from themselves. Two issues make that approach impractical for day-to-day problem solving:

1. **It is difficult to bring them in.** It takes time and effort to involve extreme outsiders—where, exactly, does one find balloon-animal artists on short notice? Therefore, many people just drop the idea for all but the most vexing, do-or-die problems.

2. **It requires high effort to communicate.** In order to reap the benefits, teams first need to bridge some pretty serious gaps of culture and communication to connect extreme outsiders to the problem.

In contrast, Charlotte was not an extreme outsider. She was an example of what management scholar Michael Tushman calls *boundary spanners*: people who understand but are not fully part of your world. Tushman argues that boundary spanners are useful exactly because they have both the internal and the external perspective. Charlotte was different enough from the management team to be capable of challenging their thinking. But at the same time, she was also close enough to understand its priorities and speak its language—and crucially, she was available to get involved on short notice.

Getting outside input is always a balancing act between urgency and effort. With big, bet-the-firm problems, or in situations where you need completely novel thinking, you should invest serious effort in getting a truly diverse group involved. But in the many cases where that's not an option, think about what else you can do to get *some* kind of outside perspective on your challenge.

Ask for input, not solutions

As you may have noticed, Charlotte didn't try to provide the group with a solution. Rather, she made an observation *that helped the managers themselves* rethink the problem.

This pattern is typical. By definition, outsiders are not experts on the situation and thus will rarely be able to solve the problem. That's not their function. They are there to stimulate the problem owners to think differently. What that means is, when you bring in outsiders:

- **Explain why they are invited.** It helps if everyone understands that they are there to help challenge assumptions and avoid blind spots.

- **Prepare the problem owners to listen.** Tell them to look for input, rather than expect solutions.

- **Ask the outsiders specifically to challenge the group's thinking.** Make it clear that they are not necessarily expected to provide solutions.

One other useful effect of having outsiders involved: it forces the problem owners to explain their problem in a different way. Sometimes, the mere act of having to restate a problem in less specialized terms can prompt experts to think differently about it.

three tactical challenges

When you use reframing, three common complications sometimes will arise. Here's advice for dealing with each:

1. Choosing which frame to focus on

Sometimes, reframing will generate many possible ways to frame the problem. To narrow down the list of frames worth focusing on, keep an eye out for framings that are:

- **Surprising.** Explore surprising problem frames; the surprise arises because the framing challenges a mental model.

- **Simple.** Prioritize simple problem frames; for most daily problems, good solutions are rarely complex. Use Occam's razor: simple answers are usually the right ones.

- **Significant-if-true.** Consider problem frames that would be highly impactful if they were true, even if your intuition suggests they aren't correct. Remember the Bolsa Familia program.

Keep in mind that you won't always have to narrow it down to just one frame. It will sometimes be possible to explore two or three framings concurrently.

2. Identifying unknown causes of a problem

When you have no clue what's causing a problem, one approach is to broadcast the problem widely (we covered this in chapter 6). Two other things you can try:

- **Use discovery-oriented conversations.** The founders of Sir Kensington solved the ketchup sales mystery through conversations, focusing on listening and learning. Who can you talk to in order to learn more?

- **Run a learning experiment.** Nickelodeon's Miah Zinn solved the app sign-up problem by inviting a few kids into the office, instead of relying on A/B testing. In the same way, can you try experimenting with a new behavior, opening the door to new insights?

3. Overcoming silo thinking

In the Marc Granger story, Charlotte's presence and her willingness to challenge the management team proved crucial. To draw on the power of outside voices, do this:

- **Use boundary spanners.** Involving "extreme" outsiders can be powerful, but doing so is not always feasible. Luckily, less can often do it. Using partial outsiders (or "boundary spanners") like Charlotte can provide much of the benefit at a fraction of the effort.

- **Ask for input, not solutions.** Outsiders aren't there to provide solutions, but to ask questions and challenge the group's thinking. Remind everyone about this as you kick off the discussion.

when people resist reframing

RESISTANCE AND DENIAL

Intransigent object
(your client)

Unstoppable force

Say you have to help someone else with their problem. If you are lucky, trust exists between you and the owner of the problem: your client regards you as a trusted adviser. Your colleague respects your expertise. Your friend knows you have their best interests at heart. All this makes it easier to challenge people's understanding of a problem.

Unfortunately, it's not always so. Here are some more typical scenarios:

- Clients may trust your expertise, yet doubt your competence in other areas: *He's a great designer, but what does he know about strategy?*

- They may be cautious about conflicts of interest: *She's just trying to generate extra business for herself. Typical consultant!*

- They may think of your role differently than you do: *As a vendor, you are here to provide solutions.*

- With colleagues, status differences can complicate the process: *Who's this upstart to question my authority?*

- And of course, the person may simply be in denial about their problem: *I'm a great listener, so don't try to tell me otherwise.*

All of these will make it harder for you to reframe the problem. In this chapter, I'll tell you how to deal with two common forms of client resistance:

- **Resistance to the process:** when people don't recognize the need for reframing

- **Denial:** when people embrace the process—yet still reject the specific diagnosis you arrive at

For simplicity, I've mostly used *client* to refer to the problem owner in the following. The advice applies equally to friends, bosses, business partners, and others—or, for that matter, to fellow team members, if you are part of a group that faces a shared problem.

RESISTANCE TO THE PROCESS

How do you make sure reframing happens when someone else controls the agenda? Here are some things you can try.

Show up with a well-designed, formal-looking framework

I generally recommend a fairly informal, organic approach to reframing. However, formalized frameworks have one great advantage: they help create legitimacy with clients.

Many design agencies rely on this tactic. Take a look at their websites, which often feature professionally designed process charts explaining their methodology. When clients see a structured, professional-looking framework, they're typically more accepting of the need to explore the problem.

The reframing canvas is one such tool you can consider using. If you do a lot of problem solving, you can consider creating your own framework, customized for the types of problems you typically work with. (Remember to let a designer touch it up be-

fore putting it in front of clients—it's a worthwhile investment.)

Educate them in advance

Prior to meeting a potential skeptic, send them a copy of this book or a copy of my *Harvard Business Review* article "Are You Solving the Right Problems?" (or any other book or article about reframing that you like). Even if they don't read what you send them, just having shared it will lend credence to the need for the process.

Share the slow elevator story

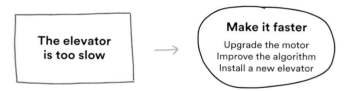

If you can't educate the client in advance, consider sharing the slow elevator problem. It's easy to memorize and takes little time to share. Sometimes, this can be enough to get clients to see the value of reframing.

Tell stories from other clients

Some clients hate being told what to do, no matter how gently you share your advice. In such cases, it can help to share stories about other companies or people, letting the clients themselves make the connection to their own situation.

Famously, the innovation expert Clayton Christensen used this method when he met Intel's CEO, Andy Grove.* Knowing that CEOs rarely like to be told what to do, Christensen didn't give direct advice when Grove solicited his opinion. Instead, Christensen said, *Well, let me tell you what I saw over at this other industry . . .* By sharing a few stories, Christensen made his point to Grove better than he would have had he directly proffered a recommendation. (This method can also work when people are in denial about the diagnosis, by the way.)

Frame the need according to their focus

Promotion — Play to win   Prevention — Play to not lose

As described in the research of Columbia University professor E. Tory Higgins, people differ in how they evaluate new ideas. Some have a *promotion focus*: they are motivated to act when there are things to be gained. Others have what's called a *prevention focus*: they are concerned with avoiding failure and losses.

This can play into how you position the need for reframing. Based on your experience with the people in question, you might try one tack or the other:

---

*Clayton Christensen is widely considered one of the foundational thinkers in the management space. He created the disruptive innovation paradigm and cocreated the jobs-to-be-done approach, a framework that many rely on to better understand and reframe customer needs.

Promotion focus. "We can't play the same game as our competitors if we want to become number one in this market. Remember how Apple suddenly became the world's biggest player in cellphones by focusing on software instead of hardware? Could we pull a similar move by rethinking what problem we're solving?"

Prevention focus. "I'm concerned that we might be solving the wrong problem. Remember how Nokia focused on building better hardware for its cellphones when it was really about the software? Are we about to make a similar mistake here?"

Manage the emotions of the process

Clients may say they don't have time to reframe, but often, it's really about their emotions, not time. To manage that situation, it's useful to know about what psychologists call *closure avoidance*, a spectrum of behavior with two extremes:

- **Closure-avoidant** people dislike having to move forward early, even if it's just a small step. *This feels very rushed to me. We need more data before we're ready to act.* Unless they manage those emotions, they can easily let a problem-solving process drag on too long.

- **Closure-seeking** people find it unnatural to have to keep more than one potential problem in mind: *Why are we still talking about this? We've got an explanation that seems to fit. Let's get mov-*

ing! Their discomfort with ambiguity and reflection leads them to jump too quickly into solution mode.

Regardless of which type of people you're working with, their emotions may thwart the process. It can help if you explain the rapid, iterative nature of the reframing process to them, and how it's designed to manage the tension between thinking and acting. On the one hand, having a process for reframing ensures that the necessary questioning is not shut down by overly action-addicted people. On the other hand, by limiting the duration of the reframing process to a manageable period, and by always ending with forward movement, the risk of paralysis by analysis is minimized.

They still may express frustration. I tell clients this: frustration is an unavoidable part of problem solving, and you should not try to repress it. It's much better to be frustrated now than later, after you have spent half a year either running in the wrong direction (the closure seekers) or doing pretty much nothing at all (closure avoiders).

The above tactics rely on overtly convincing the client to spend time on reframing. If that turns out to be hard, there are other, subtler ways of making it happen.

Invite outsiders

Sometimes, to get reframing efforts off the ground, it's better to control the guest list than the process. Can you bring somebody into the room whose perspective may help the client understand the problem differently? (See also the section on silo thinking, in chapter 10.)

Gather problem statements in advance

With groups, it can help to get their problem definitions in advance. Consider emailing each team member individually, with something like, "Hi, John! We're going to discuss our employee-engagement numbers next week. Could I get you to shoot me a few lines about what you think the problem is?"

Once you have the statements, print them out and show them in the meeting. (You can consider not attributing names to the statements if you think that will help the discussion.) This is a powerful way to start the discussion, as it will immediately become clear to everyone that they have different views of the problem.

Do it later in the process

Reframing is iterative. If you ultimately can't get the client to explore the problem up front, there may be a chance to try again later, once you've had time to gather more information.

DEALING WITH DENIAL

In my own reframing work, I've noticed a theme: *We often fall in love with problem framings that allow us not to change.* If you believe the problem is your partner's immutable personality, your company's risk-averse culture, the state of the world economy, or the unreasonably inflexible laws of physics—well, there's not much you can do about those things. And being incapable of acting can be a quietly comfortable state of affairs.

Sometimes, more-actionable framings are readily apparent—or even screamingly obvious, to outside observers at least. Why would you reject a diagnosis that, to others, is clearly correct? Here are some reasons:

- **The framing would force you to face up to an unpleasant truth.** Many nineteenth-century doctors were reluctant to recognize the importance of washing their hands—because if it turned out that disease-carrying germs actually existed, the doctors would have to face the fact that they had inadvertently caused the death of many of their own patients.

- **The framing points to a solution you want to avoid.** Someone with a drinking problem, for instance, might refuse the diagnosis in order to avoid treatment.

- **The framing runs counter to other incentives in play.** A politician might be drawn, consciously or not, to an incorrect problem framing because it promotes the interests of her constituents—or, more problematically, her financial sponsors. The writer Upton Sinclair put it well: "It is difficult to get a man to understand something, when his salary depends upon his not understanding it!"

Not all of these issues can be solved via reframing, but the method can help bring them to light. And in many cases, there are things you can do. Here's some advice on what to do if your client is in denial and rejects your diagnosis.

First, ask yourself: Could I be wrong?

The mirror of wrongness

When you're an adviser, it's always tempting to think you are right and the client wrong: *They just resist because they are stupid.* Such certainty can be seductive—but research shows that you can feel utterly certain about something and still be wrong about it.

Before launching into a campaign to overcome the client's denial, take a second to ask yourself: *Could I be wrong about this?* Sometimes, resistance on the client side is a sign of something important that they know, even if they aren't capable of putting it into words.

Then, reframe your own problem

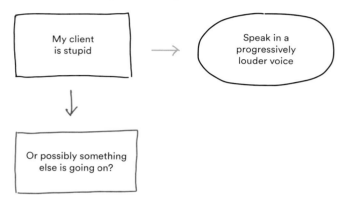

My client is stupid → Speak in a progressively louder voice

Or possibly something else is going on?

Say you remain confident in your diagnosis. Before you jump into solution mode, consider if you are understanding the problem of denial correctly. Is the client really just being unreasonable? Or might something else be going on? Here are some examples of how you can reframe the problem of denial:

Look outside the frame. Are there elements of the situation you're not aware of? Remember how Rosie Yakob (chapter 8) faced a client who rejected her advice, not because the client was irrational but because she stood to lose her bonus if the YouTube video didn't go viral.

Rethink the goal. Do you actually need the stakeholders' approval, or are there ways to achieve your (or their) goals without having to convince them? In other situations, maintaining the relationship may be more important than fixing the immediate problem.

Look in the mirror. In some cases, people resist reframing because of something *you're* doing. Maybe you aren't hiding your condescension toward the client as well as you think. Or perhaps you've missed a key concern of the client's, requiring you to spend more time understanding them. As always, when you run into a problem, question your own possible role in creating it.

Let data do the talking

Instead of trying to convince the client yourself, can you dig up data that does the job for you? Remember how Chris Dame used data from employee interviews to convince his client that bad incentives, and not bad usability, were behind the poor adoption of its new software.

Incidentally, Chris Dame also shared a classic anecdote with me about the power of data: back in the days of floppy disks, a team built a new computer. It included an exhaust vent that looked fairly similar to the slot on a floppy-disk drive. A consultant tried to convince them that users might mistake the exhaust vent for the slot, but the engineers were certain that none of their users would ever be that stupid. So the consultant gathered some data: he filmed the company's CEO trying to use the prototype. He then returned to the engineers with a video of their own CEO trying, several times, to jam a floppy disk into the exhaust vent.

Embrace their logic—and then find the weak point

Sometimes, clients reject your perspective because they firmly believe in another framing of the problem. In that case, try to *embrace* their logic—and then look for inconsistencies in their reasoning that you can point out.

Steve de Shazer (the therapist who championed short-form therapy) described a memorable example of this. One of de Shazer's clients, a war veteran, had worked for the CIA earlier in his career. The client was happily married with two kids—but he had, of late, become increasingly paranoid, believing that the CIA wanted to assassinate him. Two rear-endings of his car, occurring six weeks apart, weren't accidents to him—they were two deliberate attempts on his life. He had also taken apart the family's television, looking for hidden microphones. And most disturbingly to his wife, he had started patrolling their house at night carrying a loaded gun.

De Shazer knew it was futile to try to convince the man that the CIA wasn't out to get him. The man's wife had tried that for the last year and a half, to no avail. So de Shazer took a different approach:

> . . . the first step is to accept [the client's] beliefs at face value: behave as if there were a CIA plot against

him. Then, think about what is wrong about the details of his description of the CIA's plot. Most simply, what is wrong with the details is that the two attempts at his life had failed miserably: the CIA had not even come close to killing him. How come? When the CIA plans to kill someone, they do it. Therefore, the question is: Why would the CIA send such incompetent killers?

Notably, de Shazer didn't wield the failed assassinations as a cudgel: *So clearly you are wrong!* Instead, he simply pointed out the issue: *Isn't it weird that they haven't already killed you? I mean, you were in the CIA. If they wanted someone dead, that person would be dead now, right?* He invited the client to think about it until their next session, and then changed the subject. This, with some other interventions, eventually cured the man of his delusions.

The point, according to de Shazer, is to *introduce doubt* about the current framing rather than rejecting it outright. Then, allow the client to reach the natural conclusion himself.

Prepare two solutions

Sometimes, clients insist on getting the solution they ask for. In that case, you can consider building their solution *and* the solution you believe is best. This is a higher-risk approach, typically viable only if the second solution does not require too much time and effort to build.

Solution demanded by client

Backup solution that actually works

Regardless of the cost, this has to be done very carefully. Never forget that clients *do* know their problems better than you do, even if they aren't fully capable of explaining them well.

Let them fail once

If clients won't listen to reason, letting them fail can provide a short, sharp lesson that sets the scene for improved future collaboration. Consider the experience of an entrepreneur we'll call Anthony, cofounder of a successful streaming service.

At one point, to expand the service to a range of new countries, Anthony and his cofounder, Justin, took funding from some new investors. They expected the new investors to be fairly passive. However, as they prepared to launch their service in the next market, the investors started to involve themselves in decision making and product planning. As Anthony told me:

> We knew from experience that you couldn't just launch our service "as is" in a new country. You first had to adapt it to the local content and consumption preferences, and to do that, we needed a budget to hire local specialists to help us and sufficient time for testing and quality assurance.

Our investors didn't want to listen to that, though. They thought it was slow and unnecessary, and pushed hard to just launch the service immediately. They had been successful in other ventures and were very competent, so they came in with a bit of an attitude toward us: *We'll show these slow-moving guys how to do it.*

Anthony knew that this was the wrong choice—but he also recognized that a power battle would risk souring their relationship. More important, if Anthony got his way, there would be no proof that the investors were wrong. So he deliberately let them try it.

> The country launch wasn't do-or-die: if we failed the first time, we could still try again later. So I simply let the investors have it their way. And sure enough, the launch failed. They were smart people, but they were overconfident in this case, and failing helped them realize it.

After that, the investors approved the budgets needed to expand into new markets the right way. And just as important, they gained more respect for Anthony and Justin's hard-won experience, turning them all into a stronger team.

This tactic obviously has limitations: if the first failure would be very costly or cause harm, you can't afford to treat it as a learning experience. But if some failure isn't too costly, it may well be worth paying the price for it, seeing it as an investment in building a better relationship. Some people just need to run into the wall once or twice before they'll let you tell them where the door is.

Win the next battle instead

Some years ago, Samsung created a European innovation unit to identify disruptive ideas and sell them to the decision makers in Samsung's HQ in Korea. But as the unit's leader, Luke Mansfield, told me:

> There was very little risk willingness in Korea when it came to trying disruptive ideas. So instead of pushing harder for those, we instead started giving them much safer ideas that, while less impactful, helped them build their careers. Eventually, they trusted us enough to let us sell them on bigger ideas, allowing us to successfully deliver on our mandate.

As professionals, we understandably want to get it right every time. But sometimes, the right choice is to accept defeat and take the long view instead, building trust with the client until your voice carries more weight with them.

when people resist reframing

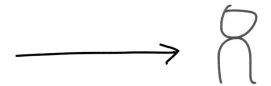

Resistance to the process

If people don't want to spend time on reframing, try one or more of the following:

- Bring a formal-looking framework.

- Educate them in advance—for instance, by sending some reading materials.

- Share the slow elevator story in the meeting.

- Tell stories from other clients.

- Pitch it according to their focus: Are they oriented toward winning or toward not losing?

- Explicitly address their emotions (closure avoidance or closure seeking).

- Invite outsiders and let them do the job for you.

- Gather problem statements in advance.

If none of that works, you can postpone the reframing work, or do it under the radar.

Dealing with denial

If people are in denial about certain aspects of the problem, here are some things you can try:

- Start by asking yourself: Could I be wrong? A client's resistance to a specific diagnosis isn't always just denial. It might indicate something you haven't taken into account.

- Consider reframing the problem of denial—is something else going on?

- Get data you can show. Can you gather some kind of evidence that can help the client see what's going on?

- Embrace their logic—and then find a weak point. Remember de Shazer's story: Why would the CIA send such incompetent killers?

- Prepare two solutions. Sometimes, it's possible to design a solution that caters both to the stated problem and to the problem you think is the better one to address.

- Let them fail once, if the downside isn't too big.

- Win the next battle instead: focus on maintaining the relationship.

a word in parting

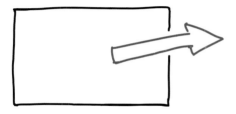

To end our journey together, I'd like to go back in time to introduce you to a special character from the late nineteenth century: Thomas C. Chamberlin.

Chamberlin, a geologist, was one of the first modern thinkers to warn against the danger of falling in love with your own theory. As he wrote in a *Science* article from 1890, back when academic journals still allowed for evocative language:

> The mind lingers with pleasure upon the facts that fall happily into the embrace of the theory, and feels a natural coldness toward those that seem refractory. Instinctively there is a special searching-out of phenomena that support it, for the mind is led by its desires.

Today we call this confirmation bias, and its corrosive effect on good judgment has been amply verified by the field of behavioral economics. Once you fall in love with your theory (Chamberlin compared it to parental affection), you risk becoming fatally blind to its flaws.

FROM THEORY TO WORKING HYPOTHESIS

The danger of confirmation bias was recognized by the scientific community in Chamberlin's time. Many of his colleagues advocated for a new concept, the *working hypothesis*, to solve the problem.

Compared with a theory, a working hypothesis was cast as a temporary explanation. Its chief purpose was to serve as a guiding framework for further research, allowing you to identify ways of testing your idea. Until such testing was conducted, the hypothesis would be treated with due caution. Today, we would say "hold your opinions lightly."

It appeared to be sound advice. Chamberlin, however, didn't embrace the working hypothesis. He knew from experience that *as long as you consider only one explanation*, however tentatively, you will be vulnerable to the intellectual equivalent of falling in love with it. There is no escaping the propensity to love an only child. So what can be done?

The solution Chamberlin proposed was to create *multiple working hypotheses*—that is, you simultaneously explore several different explanations for what might be going on. By doing this up front, you inoculate yourself against the danger of a single perspective. This should sound familiar: pursuing multiple working hypotheses is similar to the idea of looking for more than one framing of a problem when you first encounter it.

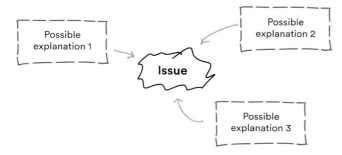

Chamberlin offered an approach for how to avoid confirmation bias. I've summarized the approach here, as it's directly applicable to how you reframe problems:

- Never commit to just one explanation up front.

- Explore multiple explanations simultaneously until sufficient empirical testing has revealed the best choice.

- Be open to the idea that the best fit may be a mix of several different explanations.

- Be prepared to walk away if something better comes along later.

Chamberlin's observations are valid for today's problems as well.

- When faced with an issue, we immediately start looking for explanations: *What's going on here? What's causing this mess?*

- More often than not, our minds come up with an answer that seems to fit the bill: *30 percent of shelter dogs are handed over by their own family? Clearly, the explanation is that they are bad people.*

- And from there on out, all bets are off as solution mode takes over. *People like that really shouldn't be allowed to adopt pets. How can we tighten our adoption processes to screen out bad owners?*

That simple flow—from pain point to problem to bad solution—causes much of our misery and wasted potential. The cure, as Chamberlin suggests, isn't to analyze our favorite theory more carefully, or to pretend that we can approach it more objectively. The cure is to come up with other viewpoints at the beginning so we avoid falling in love with a bad idea—and to remember that problems almost always have more than one solution.

I hope this book has given you the tools to start doing that. To conclude, I want to share two pieces of advice about what to do next, once you put this book down.

First, I suggest that you **start practicing the method as much as possible**. Chamberlin pointed out that with enough practice, it starts becoming an automatic habit of mind: "Instead of a simple succession of thoughts in linear order," he wrote, "the mind appears to become possessed of the power of simultaneous vision from different standpoints."

To get there, start using the method on problems big and small, at work, at home, and for that matter on social or global issues that you care about. The more you practice reframing, the better you become at using it when it really matters.

Second, I recommend that you **share the method with at least one other person in your life**. Problems grow smaller when you have someone at your side—and that is doubly true if that someone happens to understand reframing, too. Here are some ideas:

- Share it with your team, so they know what is happening (and can help) when you start talking about the need to reframe a joint problem.

- Outside of work, share it with your significant other or a good friend—whoever you turn to when you have problems you need to discuss. Share it, too, with people who rely on you for help with their own problems.

- Start a conversation with your boss, your HR team, or whoever has the power to make reframing more widely known within your workplace.

- And if you think this book deserves a wider audience, please consider writing an online review or share it some other way.

And with that, dear reader, we've come to the end of the elevator ride. We have known about the power of reframing since Chamberlin's time at least—and yet, most people *still* aren't that good at it. I think that's insane, and I think we can change it.

So let's get started.

Thomas Wedell-Wedellsborg
New York City

recommended reading

RESOURCES AND TRAINING OPTIONS

The book's website, www.howtoreframe.com, offers additional resources:

- A theory primer

- Checklists

- Print-friendly versions of the reframing canvas

- and more

The site also has information on **keynotes, training workshops**, and **large-scale licensing options** if you want to roll out reframing more widely in your organization.

READINGS ON REFRAMING

The following is a personal selection, not a definitive list. I have generally prioritized practical books. If theory is your thing, check out the book's website.

If you read only one book, go with Chip and Dan Heath's *Decisive: How to Make Better Choices in Life and Work* (New York: Crown Business, 2013). The book covers problem solving and decision making more broadly and is an excellent complement to this book. Like their previous books *Made to Stick* and *Switch*, *Decisive* is research-based, entertaining, and highly pragmatic.

Reframing in business in general

Get hold of Jennifer Riel and Roger L. Martin's book *Creating Great Choices: A Leader's Guide to Integrative Thinking* (Boston: Harvard Business Review Press, 2017). Building on Roger Martin's body of work, the authors provide helpful advice on how to work with mental models and invent new options.

Reframing in medicine

Lisa Sanders's *Every Patient Tells a Story: Medical Mysteries and the Art of Diagnosis* (New York: Broadway Books, 2009) is written for laypeople and provides a fascinating window into the field of medical diagnosis.

Reframing in politics

Jonathan Haidt's *The Righteous Mind: Why Good People Are Divided by Politics and Religion* (New York: Pantheon, 2012) offers a rich look at how conservative and progressive voters frame problems differently.

Reframing in design

Kees Dorst's *Frame Innovation: Create New Thinking by Design* (Cambridge, MA: Massachusetts Institute of Technology, 2015) offers an in-depth study of how reframing plays a central role in the practice of design. The book's theoretical discussion is particularly strong.

Reframing in negotiations

The classic **Getting to Yes: Negotiating Agreement Without Giving In** (Boston: Houghton Mifflin, 1981), by Roger Fisher, William Ury, and Bruce Patton, is still the first book you should read on the topic. The second is **Difficult Conversations: How to Discuss What Matters Most** (New York: Penguin, 1999), by Douglas Stone, Bruce Patton, and Sheila Heen. The book offers many examples of how problems are solved by getting a new perspective on the motivations of other people. The third book is **Never Split the Difference: Negotiating as if Your Life Depended on It** (New York: Harper-Collins, 2016), by former hostage negotiator Chris Voss.

Reframing in education

Teachers seeking to make their students better at questioning should consider Dan Rothstein and Luz Santana's **Make Just One Change: Teach Students to Ask Their Own Questions** (Cambridge, MA: Harvard Education Press, 2011). The book, based on Rothstein and Santana's work at the Right Question Institute, provides a detailed guide on how to work with their question formulation technique in the classroom.

Reframing in engineering and operations

The best guide here is a textbook, **Strategies for Creative Problem Solving,** 3rd ed. (Upper Saddle River, NJ: Pearson Education, 2014), by H. Scott Fogler, Steven E. LeBlanc, and Benjamin Rizzo. The book also provides an overview of the most common problem-solving frameworks.

Reframing in math and computation

For people who like their books with a solid helping of math equations, the go-to resource is Zbigniew Michalewicz and David B. Fogel's **How to Solve It: Modern Heuristics,** 2nd ed. (Berlin: Springer-Verlag, 2000), which delves into statistical methods, computational algorithms, and much more.

Reframing in startups and problem validation

Stanford University professor Steve Blank's work on customer development contains much helpful advice for diagnosing and validating customer problems. For detailed guidance, read **The Startup Owner's Manual: The Step-by-Step Guide for Building a Great Company** (Pescadero, CA: K&S Ranch Publishing, 2012), by Blank and Bob Dorf. For a quick overview, read Blank's article **"Why the Lean Start-Up Changes Everything,"** *Harvard Business Review*, May 2013. Also useful is Eric Ries's **The Lean Startup: How Today's Entrepreneurs Use Continuous Innovation to Create Radically Successful Businesses** (New York: Crown Business, 2011).

Reframing in coaching

For people who want to get better at coaching, I strongly recommend Michael Bungay Stanier's **The Coaching Habit: Say Less, Ask More, and Change the**

Way You Lead Forever (Toronto: Box of Crayons Press, 2016), a short, hands-on guide to asking questions that help clients (or yourself) rethink problems.

Reframing in reward systems

While not addressing reframing directly, Steve Kerr's short, hands-on book *Reward Systems: Does Yours Measure Up?* (Boston: Harvard School Publishing, 2009) contains some very helpful advice on how to make sure your reward systems take aim at the right problems.

Reframing in customer needs research

The jobs-to-be-done framework provides a helpful tool for understanding and rethinking customer needs and pain points. *Competing Against Luck: The Story of Innovation and Customer Choice* (New York: HarperCollins, 2016), by Clayton Christensen, Taddy Hall, Karen Dillon, and David S. Duncan, gives a comprehensive overview of the method and how to use it. For practitioners, I also recommend *Jobs to Be Done: A Roadmap for Customer-Centered Innovation* (New York: Amacom, 2016), by Stephen Wunker, Jessica Wattman, and David Farber.

Another read with a strong organizational focus is *Discovery-Driven Growth: A Breakthrough Process to Reduce Risk and Seize Opportunity* (Boston: Harvard Business Review Press, 2009), by Rita Gunther McGrath and Ian C. MacMillan.

For a useful article on questioning and reframing's role in product development, read Kevin Coyne, Patricia Gorman Clifford, and Renée Dye's **"Breakthrough Thinking from Inside the Box,"** *Harvard Business Review*, December 2007.

For a deeper dive into what's called sense-making and other ethnographic methods, read Christian Madsbjerg and Mikkel B. Rasmussen's *The Moment of Clarity: Using the Human Sciences to Solve Your Toughest Business Problems* (Boston: Harvard Business Review Press, 2014). Madsbjerg and Rasmussen are advocates for a thorough immersion into the world of the consumer, providing some convincing case studies from LEGO and elsewhere. For a quick overview, read their article **"An Anthropologist Walks into a Bar . . . ,"** *Harvard Business Review*, March 2014.

OTHER TOPICS

Questioning

The ability to ask good questions is closely related to reframing. Some good reads are:

Hal Gregersen's book *Questions Are the Answer: A Breakthrough Approach to Your Most Vexing Problems at Work and in Life* (New York: HarperCollins, 2018) and his article **"Bursting the CEO Bubble,"** *Harvard Business Review*, March–April 2017.

Warren Berger's book *A More Beautiful Question: The Power of Inquiry to Spark Breakthrough Ideas* (New York: Bloomsbury USA, 2014), which is written for a broader audience.

Edgar H. Schein's book *Humble Inquiry: The Gentle Art of Asking Instead of Telling* (San Francisco: Berrett-Koehler Publishers, 2013), a useful take, aimed at managers.

Problem solving for consultants

For those who want more depth on analytical problem solving as it's used by management consultants, read *Bulletproof Problem Solving: The One Skill That Changes Everything* (Hoboken, NJ: John Wiley & Sons, 2018), by Charles Conn and Robert McLean.

Another powerful read is *The Power of Positive Deviance: How Unlikely Innovators Solve the World's Toughest Problems* (Boston: Harvard Business Press, 2010), by Richard Pascale, Jerry Sternin, and Monique Sternin, which contains central lessons in how to create ownership of a solution within a group or community (namely by letting others frame the problems and discover the solutions themselves, with the consultant as facilitator).

Problem formulation

Before reframing problems, you first need to frame them—that is, create a problem statement. For detailed advice on formulating problems (versus reframing them), read these two articles:

Dwayne Spradlin's **"Are You Solving the Right Problem?"** *Harvard Business Review*, September 2012, which provides some helpful guidelines on how to create problem statements that allow outsiders to offer input or solutions.

Nelson P. Repenning, Don Kieffer, and Todd Astor's **"The Most Underrated Skill in Management,"** *MIT Sloan Management Review*, Spring 2017, which provides some helpful advice on how to clarify goals in particular.

Influence tactics

If your main challenge is to influence others—for instance, if you need to bring a team around to considering your point of view—read Phil M. Jones's short book *Exactly What to Say: The Magic Words for Influence and Impact* (Box of Tricks Publishing, 2017), which provides very tactical advice on what phrases to employ.

Another classic read is Robert Cialdini's *Influence: The Psychology of Persuasion* (get the revised edition from HarperBusiness, 2006).

Understanding yourself and others

For a short guide aimed at practitioners, read Heidi Grant Halvorson's *No One Understands You and*

What to Do About It (Boston: Harvard Business Review Press, 2015). For a deeper dive, read Tasha Eurich's ***Insight: The Surprising Truth About How Others See Us, How We See Ourselves, and Why the Answers Matter More Than We Think*** (New York: Currency, 2017).

The art of observation

As in a Sherlock Holmes story, successful problem solving can sometimes hinge on the ability to see something that others don't notice. If you are looking to upgrade your observational skills, I recommend Amy E. Herman's book ***Visual Intelligence: Sharpen Your Perception, Change Your Life*** (New York: Houghton Mifflin Harcourt, 2016). Through the study of classical artworks, Herman has taught the art of observation to FBI agents and police officers, and her book includes color illustrations that readers can use to sharpen their ability to see what others miss.

Diversity

My favorite book on diversity is Scott Page's ***The Diversity Bonus: How Great Teams Pay Off in the Knowledge Economy*** (Princeton, NJ: Princeton University Press, 2017), which shares both the evidence for the advantages of diversity and some helpful frameworks for using diversity optimally.

Mental models and metaphor theory

The impact of mental models and metaphors on our thinking cannot be overestimated. For those with an interest in cognition and linguistics, I recommend Douglas Hofstadter and Emmanuel Sander's ***Surfaces and Essences: Analogy as the Fuel and Fire of Thinking*** (New York: Basic Books, 2013), as well as the still-interesting classic by George Lakoff and Mark Johnson, ***Metaphors We Live By*** (Chicago: University of Chicago Press, 1980).

notes

Introduction: what's your problem?

Page 4: **More than fifty years' of research.** What I refer to as "reframing" in this book has a variety of names in the research literature, including "problem finding," "problem discovery," "problem formulation," "problem construction," and others. The primary concentration of scientific research into reframing has taken place within the field of creativity studies, starting with the empirical explorations of Jacob Getzels and Mihaly Csikszentmihalyi in 1971, and continuing through the contributions of scholars such as Michael Mumford, Mark Runco, Robert Sternberg, Roni Reiter-Palmon, and many others.

The full history of reframing, however, is much broader than that. Problem diagnosis is central to pretty much any theoretical and practical discipline you care to mention, and as a consequence, you'll find thinkers on reframing in almost any area of human endeavor. An incomplete timeline of some select early reframing thinkers and their fields would include geology (Chamberlin, 1890), education (Dewey, 1910), psychology (Duncker, 1935), physics (Einstein and Infeld, 1938), math (Polya, 1945), operations management (Ackoff, 1960), philosophy (Kuhn, 1962), critical theory (Foucault, 1966), sociology (Goffman, 1974), behavioral economics (Kahneman and Tversky, 1974), and not least management science (Drucker, 1954; Levitt, 1960; Argyris, 1977). Adding to that, central contributions have also been made by practitioners from fields such as entrepreneurship, coaching, negotiations, business strategy, behavior design, conflict resolution, and in particular, design thinking.

If you want to delve deeper into the history of reframing, see this book's website (www.howtoreframe.com) where I've provided a fuller overview of the scientific evidence behind the concept, including complete references for the reframing thinkers mentioned in this note.

4: **Not that hard to learn.** The idea that reframing is a teachable skill (and not just an innate talent) is backed by research. A 2004 meta-study (meaning a review of all the available research) found that training in problem finding is one of the most effective ways of making people more creative; see Ginamarie Scott, Lyle E. Leritz, and Michael D. Mumford, "The Effectiveness of Creativity Training: A Quantitative Review," *Creativity Research Journal* 16, no. 4 (2004): 361.

5: **The slow elevator problem.** The elevator story is a classic anecdote whose exact point of origin—if there is one—has been lost to history. To my knowledge, the first academic reference was in a 1960 paper by the noted operations researcher Russell L. Ackoff, who shared it to highlight the need for interdisciplinary problem-solving teams; see Ackoff, "Systems, Organizations, and Interdisciplinary Research," *General Systems*, vol. 5 (1960). Ackoff himself referred to the story as anecdotal in his later writings. I thank Arundhita Bhanjdeo, as well as Elizabeth Webb and Silvia Bellezza of Columbia Business School, for pointing me to Ackoff's original paper.

5: **Put up mirrors.** Note that the mirror solution is not intended as "the answer" to the slow elevator problem. (Mirrors won't work, for instance, if the problem is that people run late for their meetings.) The mirror solution is simply a memorable example of the core idea: by reframing the problem, you can sometimes identify much better solutions than the ones you'll find through more traditional forms of problem analysis.

6: **The power of reframing has been known for decades.** One famous formulation was written in 1938 by Albert Einstein and Leopold Infeld: "The formulation of a problem is often more essential than its solution, which may be merely a matter of mathematical or experimental skill. To raise new questions, new possibilities, *to regard old problems from a new angle*, requires creative imagination and marks real advance in science." (See Einstein and Infeld, *The Evolution of Physics* [Cambridge: Cambridge University Press, 1938]. The passage appears on page 92 in the 2007 edition. Emphasis mine.) The underlying idea of solving the right problem has been around for even longer. Two early contributors were Thomas C. Chamberlin (1890) and John Dewey (1910). The term "framing" as it's used here was introduced in 1974 by the sociologist Erving Goffman in his book *Frame Analysis: An Essay on the Organization of Experience* (Boston: Harvard University Press, 1974). Goffman saw frames as mental models that we use to organize and interpret our experiences—that is, as a tool for sense-making.

7: **85 percent said that their organizations were not good at reframing.** The data comes from three surveys I conducted in 2015 with 106 senior executives that attended one of my sessions. The response patterns were consistent across all three surveys. Less than one in ten said that their company did not struggle significantly with problem diagnosis.

10: **The reframing canvas.** I owe thanks to Alexander Osterwalder and Yves Pigneur for paving the way for a new format of business books, and for serving as a partial inspiration for my creation of the reframing canvas.

10: **CEOs use reframing to great effect.** For two contemporary examples, see Roger L. Martin's body of work on integrative thinking and Hal Gregersen's work on questioning skills, listed in the recommended readings.

Chapter 1: reframing explained

14: **The most basic trait of good problem solvers is their optimism.** Starting with the work of psychologist Albert Bandura, there is a large body of scholarship on what researchers call self-efficacy—that is, the belief that "I can do it"; see Albert Bandura, "Self-Efficacy in Human Agency," *American Psychologist* 37, no. 2 (1982): 122–147. Interestingly, self-efficacy is not strictly a result of experience or learned behavior. There is some evidence that it's mostly an inherited trait; see Trine Waaktaar and Svenn Torgersen, "Self-Efficacy Is Mainly Genetic, Not Learned: A Multiple-Rater Twin Study on the Causal Structure of General Self-Efficacy in Young People," *Twin Research and Human Genetics* 16, no. 3 (2013): 651–660. Also, self-efficacy measures only the *belief* that you can succeed, and is not necessarily related to actual efficacy (that is, real-world *outcomes*). For more on this, see the following endnote as well.

14: **History is full of happy optimists running head first into walls.** For an example of how self-confidence can lead people into dead-end solutions, look no further than the research into entrepreneurship. In one fascinating study by Thomas Astebro and Samir Elhedhli, the researchers looked at entrepreneurs whose business plans had been rated as very unlikely to succeed by a nonprofit organization called the Canadian Innovation Centre. Half of these entrepreneurs disregarded the input and launched their businesses anyway. And then they failed, every single one, as predicted; see Thomas Astebro and Samir Elhedhli, "The Effectiveness of Simple Decision Heuristics: Forecasting Commercial Success for Early-Stage Ventures," *Management Science* 52, no. 3 (2006). I owe thanks to organizational psychologist Tasha Eurich for pointing me to this study via her book *Insight: The Surprising Truth about How Others See Us, How We See Ourselves, and Why the Answers Matter More Than We Think* (New York: Currency, 2017).

15: **More than three million dogs enter a shelter.** The statistics shared here are from the website of the ASPCA.

Compared with censuses of human beings, the record keeping on pets is imprecise, which is why you may see quite different numbers depending on the source.

15: **Henrik Werdelin's BarkBox story.** Personal conversation with Henrik Werdelin and Stacie Grissom, 2016.

16: **A fair amount of bark for your buck.** What impact did BarkBuddy have on shelter adoptions? The shelter contact details were listed directly on the dogs' profiles, so BarkBox didn't have a way to track adoptions made via the app. However, the $8,000 cost of building the app provides a way to assess whether it made a difference, compared to a scenario in which the BarkBox team had simply donated the $8,000 to a shelter or a rescue group. Assuming an average cost of $85 for saving one shelter dog (a number you'll see later), BarkBuddy would have made a positive difference if only about one hundred additional people adopted shelter dogs because of the app. With a million monthly page views in the period after its launch, it seems highly likely that the BarkBuddy app had a significant positive impact on adoptions.

16: **Lori Weise's shelter intervention program.** The story of Lori's work is based on several conversations I had with her from 2016 to 2018, as well as on Lori's book on the topic, *First Home, Forever Home: How to Start and Run a Shelter Intervention Program* (CreateSpace Publishing, 2015), which both details her story and explains how to run a similar program. Parts of the story were initially published in my article "Are You Solving the Right Problems?," from the January–February 2017 issue of *Harvard Business Review*. I owe thanks to Suzanna Schumacher for making me aware of Lori's story.

17: **The number of pets that end up in a shelter and the number that are euthanized are at all-time lows.** In recent years, adoption rates, shelter-intake rates, and euthanasia rates have seen dramatic positive change. From 2011 to 2017, counting both dogs and cats, adoptions have increased from 2.7 million to 3.2 million, and euthanasia has decreased from 2.6 million to 1.5 million. The shelter intervention programs—also called safety net programs—are one part of this, but many other initiatives played a part too. The indus-

try is more complicated than I can convey here. If you want to delve deeper, I recommend starting at the website of the ASPCA (www.aspca.org), which offers lots of resources. The improvement numbers quoted above are from an ASPCA press release published on March 1, 2017.

19: **Ron Adner's concept of a wide lens.** See Ron Adner's *The Wide Lens: What Successful Innovators See That Others Miss* (New York: Portfolio/Penguin, 2012). As an aside, even with all these things, the BarkBuddy app wouldn't have been possible without the prior creation, by PetFinder.com, of a central database where shelters can list their available dogs, and from which the BarkBuddy app drew its data.

20: **Paul C. Nutt's research on decision making.** As Nutt writes, "Discarded options are not wasted. They help you confirm the value of a preferred course of action and frequently offer ways to improve it." Nutt's research is summarized in his book *Why Decisions Fail: Avoiding the Blunders and Traps That Lead to Debacles* (San Francisco: Berrett-Koehler, 2002). The above quote is from page 264.

21: **The most important skills for the future.** This is from the World Economic Forum's "Future of Jobs Report 2016."

22: **Reframing has been used to find new solutions to deeply entrenched political conflicts.** The story I refer to is that of the 1978 Camp David Accords. For an in-depth discussion of how framing affects policy making, check out Carol Bacchi's work on her WPR framework. For even more in-depth (bordering on dense) discussions, see Donald A. Schön and Martin Rein's *Frame Reflection: Toward the Resolution of Intractable Policy Controversies* (New York: Basic Books, 1994).

22: **Framing can be weaponized.** The study of how framing can be used to influence opinion harks back to the early days of what's called agenda-setting research within political science. Early writings in the field focused more on how the prioritization and frequency of news coverage on a topic affected people's opinions about it. Later research started examining how different framings of a topic affected how people felt and thought about it.

If you follow US politics, one interesting guide is George Lakoff's book *Don't Think of An Elephant!: Know Your Values and Frame the Debate* (White River Junction, NJ: Chelsea Green Publishing, 2004). Lakoff is one of the seminal scholars on framing effects and their connection to language and metaphors. Note, though, that Lakoff is a self-declared liberal and isn't exactly hiding it. For a more politically balanced read, get hold of Jonathan Haidt's *The Righteous Mind: Why Good People Are Divided by Politics and Religion* (New York: Pantheon, 2012).

Another important contribution to the research on framing effects comes from Daniel Kahneman and Amos Tversky's seminal studies of how framing leads us to vastly different conclusions, based—for instance—on whether we perceive a change to represent a loss or a gain. Read Kahneman's *Thinking, Fast and Slow* (New York: Farrar, Straus and Giroux, 2011) for an in-depth discussion. For a more cursory but superbly written exposition, read Michael Lewis's book *The Undoing Project: A Friendship That Changed Our Minds* (New York: W. W. Norton & Company, 2017). For an even more cursory exposition, enter any bookstore, throw a dart in the popular psychology section, and read whatever book it hits.

Chapter 2: getting ready to reframe

28: **"Thinky thoughts."** The expression was coined by Adelaide Richardson, daughter of Sheila Heen, a writer and negotiation expert you'll meet in chapter 7, "Look in the Mirror."

28: **"We don't have time to invent the wheel . . ."** Personal conversation with pharmaceutical executive Christoffer Lorenzen, over a latte, 2010.

28: **The "fifty-five minutes" quotation.** The "Einstein" quotation first appeared in a 1966 paper in which it was attributed not to Einstein but to an unnamed professor at Yale University. For a full rundown of the quotation's many permutations, see Garson O'Toole's excellent website QuoteInvestigator.com. Also, I love how even the most dubious idea becomes immune to criticism once you claim Einstein or some other luminary said it. Speaking of which, here's another quotation that was in fact attributed* to Einstein, Gandhi, Steve Jobs, Mother Teresa, and Queen Elizabeth I: "You should recommend *What's Your Problem?* to everyone you know."

29: **Reframing as a brief, iterated practice.** One of the first scholars to study how experts actually work, the MIT professor Donald Schön, talked about the idea of "reflection-in-action." See Schön's *The Reflective Practitioner: How Professionals Think in Action* (New York: Basic Books, 1983). The term captured Schön's observation that people such as teachers, architects, and health-care professionals tended to reflect on their own methods and revise them *as they worked*, rather than relying on separate, more formal theory building. (His collaborator Chris Argyris introduced similar ideas to management in his work on so-called double loop learning.) Many other experts have talked about the need to build small habits of reflection into your everyday life. I personally like management scholars Ronald Heifetz and Marty Linsky's concept of "getting onto the balcony," shared in their book *Leadership on the Line: Staying Alive through the Dangers of Leading* (Boston: Harvard Business Press, 2002). For those who like sports metaphors (if not actual sports), the reframing loop is similar to the way that brief, focused breaks are used in many sports: time-outs in basketball, huddles in American football, or pit-stop visits in Formula One racing.

32: **"Habits of mind."** Stephen Kosslyn, formerly a dean of social sciences at Harvard University, talks about habits of mind in *Building the Intentional University: Minerva and the Future of Higher Education* (Cambridge, MA: Massachusetts Institute of Technology, 2017), which he coedited with Ben Nelson.

---

*Specifically, I attributed it to them, just now.

33: **Hal Gregersen on quick applications.** The quotation is from Gregersen's article "Better Brainstorming," *Harvard Business Review*, March–April 2018, which also describes the "question burst" method.

33: **Open the door to later insights, once the questions have had some time to settle in.** You can think of reframing as both an active and a passive process. The active process is when you go through the framework. The passive part happens in the background, outside the formal process, as you work toward analyzing and solving the problem. The passive version bears strong similarity to the process of "incubation," a key component of most creativity models since the concept was introduced by the early creativity scholar Graham Wallas in 1926. In my experience, doing an initial, active round of reframing can be very helpful for "priming" people to notice anomalies and other signs that can help with the subsequent, more passive part of diagnosing the problem.

Chapter 3: frame the problem

42: **About a decade after the field of creativity research was founded.** The scientific study of creativity is considered to be officially founded in 1950, in a lecture by the psychologist J. P. Guilford. Getzels first wrote about the two problem types in chapter 3 of a 1962 book, *Creativity and Intelligence: Explorations with Gifted Students* (London; New York: Wiley), coauthored with Philip W. Jackson. (Getzels credits the contributions of two earlier thinkers, the psychologist Max Wertheimer and the mathematician Jacques Hadamard.) Getzels's later work with a fellow psychologist, Mihaly Csikszentmihalyi, is now considered foundational in the field of problem finding and reframing.

42: **Getzels called these presented problems.** According to Getzels, a presented problem is clearly stated and has a known method of solving it, and it's clear when the problem has been solved (like the Pythagoras math question). A discovered problem, in contrast, is ill-defined and may not even

be recognized. There is no known method for solving it, and it may not even be clear when the problem can be considered solved. Getzels didn't consider this to be an either-or distinction. Rather, he positioned the concepts more as opposing ends of a spectrum. For more on Getzels's work, see chapter 4 in *Perspectives in Creativity* (New York: Transaction Publishers, 1975), edited by Irving A. Taylor and Jacob W. Getzels.

42: **Pain points, problems, goals, and solutions.** The typology I use here is an amalgamation of existing frameworks. The main part is derived from what is perhaps the most widely used definition of *problem solving*, namely when someone has a goal but doesn't know how to achieve it. For a summary, see Richard E. Mayer's *Thinking, Problem Solving, Cognition*, 2nd ed. (New York: Worth Publishers, 1991). I have added the "pain point" part as well to highlight the difference between well-defined and ill-defined problems, building on Jacob Getzels's work and that of several other thinkers—such as the operations scholar Russell Ackoff's idea of "messes"; Donald J. Treffinger and Scott G. Isaksen's later work on mess-finding; and not least the even earlier education scholar John Dewey's reflections on the idea of a "felt difficulty," expressed back in 1910.

43: **Two out of three patients initially couldn't point to a specific problem.** De Shazer discusses this on page 9 of his book *Keys to Solution in Brief Therapy* (New York: W. W. Norton & Company, 1985). The number is from de Shazer's own research, conducted among fellow practitioners of what's called Solution-Focused Brief Therapy. (You'll hear more on the method in chapter 6, "Examine Bright Spots.") In my own informal conversations with psychologists, they typically put the number at between 30 percent and 60 percent, which suggests in part that the very concept of what a problem is can be fuzzy as well.

44: **A hard-to-reach goal.** The early problem-solving literature, especially within operations science, focused mostly on negative deviations from the norm—e.g., when a manufacturing line broke down. Later, the focus was expanded to include what I call here goal-driven problems—that is, situations in which people aren't necessarily unhappy with their present circumstances but nonetheless seek to improve things. For a review of the different types of "gaps" that drive problem-solving efforts, see Min Basadur, S. J. Ellspermann, and G. W. Evans, "A New Methodology for Formulating Ill-Structured Problems," *Omega* 22, no. 6 (1994): 627.

Incidentally, the shift identified by Basadur also occurred within psychology when Martin Seligman and others introduced the concept of positive psychology. In contrast to traditional psychology, which mostly concerns itself with addressing pathologies (again, negative deviations from the norm), positive psychology focuses on how to further improve the lives of people who are already functioning well.

45: **A solution in search of a problem.** In fairness, doing something new can certainly be worthwhile on occasion, even if it's not aimed at solving a specific problem. In corporate innovation, you'll often see a distinction between problem-centric and idea-centric innovation (the terms used for these will vary). Problem-centric innovation tends to have better success rates as measured by the hit-to-miss ratio. Idea-centric innovation, meaning projects that are started without any concerns about having to address an existing need or problem, is generally considered much riskier—but the few ideas that *do* manage to take off often end up having an outsize impact. For innovators and investors, this can be a worthwhile trade-off depending on their goals and risk tolerances. In the context of practical problem solving at work, though, assuming you have a regular job, I would suggest you err in the direction of targeting known problems rather than going for blue-sky initiatives.

46: **When looking at a problem statement, a good first question to ask is,** *How do we know this is true?* Among other places, this principle has been formalized within education by Dan Rothstein and Luz Santana, founders of the Right Question Institute. Their framework teaches children to "open" a question: "Why is my dad so strict?" (a closed statement) becomes "Is my dad actually strict?" (an open statement).

46: **Gregers Wedell-Wedellsborg's story from TV2.** I originally shared this story in an article I coauthored with Paddy Miller: "The Case for Stealth Innovation," *Harvard Business Review*, March 2013.

47: **Lack of knowledge prevents people from eating healthier food.** It is conceivable that the students' framing of the problem was driven by convenience (consciously or not): a communications campaign is fairly easy to gin up and roll out, whereas an effort to, say, change the menu options or rearrange the layout of the cafeteria could be more demanding. We're often tempted to frame problems so that they point in the direction of our preferred solutions (or better yet, so that they allow us not to change).

50: **Poorly framed trade-offs are classic pitfalls.** Within the field of management science, the leading contemporary thinker on framing strategic choices is arguably Roger L. Martin, former Dean of Rotman School of Management. Martin has written a number of books on what he calls "integrative thinking"—that is, the ability to generate superior options by integrating seemingly disparate options. My work draws on several of the insights offered by him and his various coauthors. If you want to delve into this, I recommend starting with *Creating Great Choices: A Leader's Guide to Integrative Thinking* (Boston: Harvard Business Review Press, 2017), coauthored with his longtime collaborator Jennifer Riel.

50: **"Nuclear war, present policy, or surrender."** See Kissinger's memoir *White House Years* (New York: Little, Brown and Co., 1979). The story is shared on page 418 of the 2011 paperback edition by Simon & Shuster. I owe thanks to Chip and Dan Heath for highlighting the quotation in their book *Decisive: How to Make Better Choices in Life and Work*.

51: **Ashley Albert story.** I have followed Ashley's entrepreneurial career for several years. The quotations are from conversations I had with her in 2018.

52: **People have much better chances of success if their goals are specific.** For a great introduction to this, read Chip and Dan Heath's book *Switch: How to Change Things*

When Change Is Hard (New York: Broadway Books, 2010), or check out the academic work of Edwin Locke and Gary Latham.

Chapter 4: look outside the frame

56: Secret writing and lemon juice. I have a sneaking suspicion that right now, somewhere out there, a reader just dipped my book in lemon juice. I commend you for your initiative and healthy disregard for authority, and I apologize for the lack of rewarding Easter eggs. Maybe in the next edition. Also, secret-writing experts may know that dipping it in lemon juice won't help. The trick is to *write* the message in lemon juice, and then reveal it by heating up the page—preferably without setting it on fire.

56: New York to Le Havre. The original story is described in the 1915 textbook *Initiation Mathematique*, by Charles-Ange Laisant, published by Hachette. I came across it in Alex Bellos's delightful book of brainteasers, *Can You Solve My Problems?: Ingenious, Perplexing, and Totally Satisfying Math and Logic Puzzles* (Norwich, UK: Guardian Books, 2016). I have revised the wording of the riddle for the sake of clarity. Incidentally, Édouard Lucas was also the inventor of the "Tower of Hanoi" puzzle, a classic challenge within the problem-solving literature.

57: We usually aren't even aware that we're not seeing the full picture. While framing is a largely subconscious process, research has shown that you can learn to become more aware of how you frame problems—and that doing so makes you more creative. See, for example, Michael Mumford, Roni Reiter-Palmon, and M. R. Redmond, "Problem Construction and Cognition: Applying Problem Representations in Ill-Defined Domains" in Mark A. Runco (ed.) *Problem Finding, Problem Solving, and Creativity* (Westport, CT: Ablex, 1994).

58: You *know* there's a catch somewhere. If you got the ship counting challenge wrong, how did you react? Some react with curiosity. Others, I've noticed, react by immedi-ately scanning the challenge for creative interpretations that allow them to claim they were in fact right. ("*Well, I thought you were asking about the company's very first day of operations!*") If that's you, here's a thought: If you are never willing to tell yourself "I got it wrong," you'll never learn. There can be strength in admitting a mistake—not necessarily in public (that's not always a good idea), but at least to yourself, to properly learn from it.

59: Kees Dorst quotation. See Kees Dorst, "The Core of 'Design Thinking' and Its Application," *Design Studies* 32, no. 6 (2011): 521.

59: Doctors don't just focus on the stated ailment. Lisa Sanders's *Every Patient Tells a Story: Medical Mysteries and the Art of Diagnosis* (New York: Broadway Books, 2009) offers a riveting collection of anecdotes along with some thought-provoking reflections on diagnosis. (You may know her writings from her Diagnosis column in the *New York Times*.) Another classic read on the topic is Jerome Groopman's *How Doctors Think* (Boston: Houghton Mifflin, 2007). Also, pretty much anything Atul Gawande has written.

59: Problem-solving experts are trained to look beyond the immediate cause of an incident. The distinction between immediate (proximate) causes and systems-level (distal or ultimate) causes is a key feature of most problem-solving frameworks within operations science, such as Six Sigma and the Toyota Production System. The systems scientist Peter Senge is often credited with introducing systems thinking (and many associated ideas) into modern management via his book *The Fifth Discipline: the Art and Practice of the Learning Organization* (New York: Currency, 1990).

59: "The law of the instrument." The quotation is from page 28 of Abraham Kaplan's *The Conduct of Inquiry: Methodology for Behavioral Science* (San Francisco: Chandler Publishing Company, 1964). Another Abraham, Abraham Maslow of the famous hierarchy of needs, is frequently cited in a similar vein: "I suppose it is tempting, if the only tool you have is a hammer, to treat everything as if it were a nail." The remark appears on page 15 of Maslow's *The Psychology of Science: A Reconnaissance* (New York: Harper & Row, 1966).

As an aside, the law of the instrument shows what a difference it can make when people find powerful metaphors with which to express their ideas. Consider the other way Kaplan expressed the law, from the same book: "It comes as no particular surprise to discover that a scientist formulates problems in a way which requires for their solution just those techniques in which he himself is especially skilled." The sentence was possibly inspired by the law of tortuously convoluted sentences, very popular in some corners of academia. I suspect Kaplan's research would have had less impact if he hadn't taken the time to come up with the metaphor of the hammer-wielding child.

60: **Senior executives in Brazil.** I originally shared this story in "Are You Solving the Right Problems?" *Harvard Business Review*, January–February 2017. Parts of the story are taken verbatim from the article.

61: **"Insanity is doing the same thing over and over . . ."** This is another quotation that's often misattributed to Albert Einstein. Michael Becker, an editor from the *Bozeman Daily Chronicle*, explores the origin of the quotation in his blog post "Einstein on Misattribution: 'I Probably Didn't Say That'" (http://www.news.hypercrit.net/2012/11/13/einstein-on-misattribution-i-probably-didnt-say-that/). As Becker points out, an early version of the quotation predates Rita Mae Brown's 1983 *Sudden Death*, namely in a text from Narcotics Anonymous. Compared to the Einstein attribution, I guess that wouldn't look as snazzy on a motivational poster.

62: **Did you remember to eat breakfast this morning?** For some US-based data on this, check out the work of the No Kid Hungry initiative (www.nokidhungry.org). For an example of a real-world application, see Jake J. Protivnak, Lauren M. Mechling, and Richard M. Smrek, "The Experience of At-Risk Male High School Students Participating in

Academic Focused School Counseling Sessions," *Journal of Counselor Practice* 7, no. 1 (2016):41–60. I owe thanks to Erin Gorski, professor at Montclair State University, for pointing me to this example.

The pattern affects adults as well. One study famously showed that a prisoner's chance of obtaining parole swings wildly depending on whether the prisoner's hearing happens before or after the parole board has eaten lunch. See Shai Danziger, Jonathan Levav, and Liora Avnaim-Pesso, "Extraneous Factors in Judicial Decisions," *Proceedings of the National Academy of Sciences* 108, no. 17 (2011).

63: **The marshmallow test.** For the original paper, see Yuichi Shoda, Walter Mischel, and Philip K. Peake, "Predicting Adolescent Cognitive and Self-Regulatory Competencies from Preschool Delay of Gratification: Identifying Diagnostic Conditions," *Developmental Psychology* 26, no. 6 (1990): 978. For the new study, see Tyler W. Watts, Greg J. Duncan, and Haonan Quan, "Revisiting the Marshmallow Test: A Conceptual Replication Investigating Links Between Early Delay of Gratification and Later Outcomes," *Psychological Science* 29, no. 7 (2018): 1159. For a quick overview, read Jessica McCrory Calarco's article "Why Rich Kids Are So Good at the Marshmallow Test," in the *Atlantic*, published online on June 1, 2018.

65: **The light bulb problem.** What if it's LED bulbs and not old-school light bulbs? The one-trip solution actually still works: while the glass of an LED bulb remains cool, the base of the bulb still gets warm after a minute or two. People who have grown up with LED bulbs, though, will likely find it harder to spot the one-trip solution, as LED bulbs are *perceived* to be heatless: a cognitive scientist might say that the "heat" property will have a harder time being activated in their minds.

There's another reason I like the light bulb problem: it highlights our deep reliance on vision as a metaphor. Note how many of our metaphors for reframing are visually based: seeing the big picture, taking a step back, getting a bird's-eye perspective, stepping onto the balcony, and indeed, "seeing" a problem differently. Relying on visual metaphors is generally a helpful shortcut—but as with all metaphors, it can also lead you astray or (pun intended) blind you to some aspects of the situation, as the light bulb problem beautifully demonstrates.

65: **Researchers call the brain a cognitive miser.** The concept was coined in 1984 by Susan Fiske and Shelley Taylor. See Fiske and Taylor, *Social Cognition: From Brains to Culture* (New York: McGraw-Hill, 1991). It is comparable to Daniel Kahneman's concept of System 1 thinking. See Kahneman, *Thinking, Fast and Slow* (New York: Farrar, Straus, and Giroux: 2011).

66: **Functional fixedness.** The concept of functional fixedness is associated with Karl Duncker, an influential early researcher of creative problem solving. Duncker's most famous contribution was the "candle test," in which participants have to affix a candle to a wall, using a box of tacks and a few other things. The canonical solution is to use the empty tack box to create a platform for the candle—that is, participants have to use the box for something different than its normal function. See K. Duncker, "On Problem Solving," *Psychological Monographs* 58, no. 5 (1945): i–113.

66: **The parking attendants at Disney.** The problem is adapted from Jeff Gray's article "Lessons in Management: What Would Walt Disney Do?" *Globe and Mail*, July 15, 2012.

Chapter 5: rethink the goal

71: **Rethinking the goal.** The notion of rethinking your goals has been explored within philosophy as well. One particularly interesting point relates to the concept of "straight-line instrumentalism" as discussed by philosopher Langdon Winner. The concept covers the idea—dubious according to Winner—that our goals exist and are formed independently of the tools we employ to reach them. Winner argues instead that our tools are part of shaping our goals as well as our values; see "Do Artifacts Have Politics?" *Daedalus* 109,

no. 1 (1980): 121–136. For problem solvers, this serves as yet another reminder to continually examine the relationship between our goals, our problems, and our tools and solutions. I owe thanks to Prehype partner Amit Lubling for making me aware of Winner's work.

73: **Goals don't really exist in isolation, as simple endpoints.** Unusually for any self-respecting academic discipline, there's actually widespread agreement on what a goal is. Edwin Locke and Gary Latham say, "A goal is the object or aim of an action"; see "Building a Practically Useful Theory of Goal Setting and Task Motivation: A 35-Year Odyssey," *American Psychologist* 57, no. 9 (2002): 705–717. Richard E. Mayer talks about the "desired or terminal state" of a problem, highlighting that goal states can be more or less fuzzy; see *Thinking, Problem Solving, and Cognition*, 2nd ed. (New York: W.H. Freeman and Company, 1992): 5–6. In practice, though, people don't use terms like *goal* and *problem* consistently. One person might say, "The problem is that sales have dropped," while another will say, "Our goal is to improve sales." Part of the job of reframing is to eventually clarify what the important goals are—which is particularly salient when you work with clients, as those goals also double as a "stopping rule" for when the work is completed. I thank Martin Reeves of Boston Consulting Group for highlighting this.

73: **Goals as part of a hierarchy or causal chain.** The idea of hierarchical goals has been explored by many different scholars and practitioners. Among these, the teacher and researcher Min Basadur deserves special mention due to his work on the "Why-What's Stopping" method, published in 1994, which this chapter is partially inspired by; see Min Basadur, S. J. Ellspermann, and G. W. Evans, "A New Methodology for Formulating Ill-Structured Problems," *Omega* 22, no. 6 (1994). Other incarnations of the approach can be found in the automotive industry, such as in Ford's "laddering" technique, or in the idea of a "jobs tree" that forms part of the jobs-to-be-done framework.

74: **The Camp David Accords.** The story is described in Roger Fisher, William Ury, and Bruce Patton's *Getting to Yes:*

Negotiating Agreement Without Giving In (Boston: Houghton Mifflin, 1981). The authors urged people to "focus on interests, not positions," a principle that has since become a core tenet in negotiations research. Credit for the original insight belongs to the early management scholar Mary Parker Follett, who described it in a 1925 paper called "Constructive Conflict"; see Pauline Graham, ed., *Mary Parker Follett— Prophet of Management* (Boston: Harvard Business School Publishing, 1995), 69. In the language I use here, *positions* equal the stated goals and *interests* equal the higher-level, possibly unstated goals.

75: **"Some people do not know how they will know when their problem is solved."** The quotation is from page 9 of Steve de Shazer's *Keys to Solution in Brief Therapy* (New York: W. W. Norton and Company, 1985).

75: **A goal map is a model of *how you think the world works.*** For a good discussion of this, see Jennifer Riel and Roger L. Martin, *Creating Great Choices: A Leader's Guide to Integrative Thinking* (Boston: Harvard Business Review Press, 2017).

75: **Career advice to young adults.** On the topic of career advice, the famous comedian Bo Burnham was once asked what advice he'd give to young people that dreamed about doing what he does. His answer? *Give up now.* As he explained (I've revised the wording a bit): *Don't take advice from people like me who have gotten very lucky. We're very biased. A superstar telling you to follow your dreams is like a lottery winner telling you, "Liquidize your assets. Buy lottery tickets. It works!"* Burnham shared this on the US talk show *Conan,* hosted by Conan O'Brien, in an episode that aired on June 28, 2016. Depending on your country's viewing restrictions, you can possibly access the clip online: search for "Bo Burnham's inspirational advice."

76: **Net-90 policy.** Personal conversation with Henrik Werdelin, 2018. Werdelin is the BarkBox cofounder you met in this book's opening.

76: **On goal models and performance metrics.** For more on how performance goals are often poorly conceived—and

how to get them right—check out Steve Kerr, *Reward Systems: Does Yours Measure Up?* (Boston: Harvard Business School Publishing, 2009), or Kerr's classic article "On the Folly of Rewarding A, While Hoping for B," *Academy of Management Journal* 18, no. 4 (1975): 769. One of my own examples is of an innovation manager whose boss made her bonus dependent on implementing at least 5 percent of the incoming ideas. That might have been a great goal if at least 5 percent of the incoming ideas were potentially good. Unfortunately, that wasn't the case, and the manager was thus forced to implement a number of bad ideas, knowing that they would be a waste of time.

76: **Anna Ebbesen on assumptions.** Personal conversation with Anna Ebbesen, May 2019. Ebbesen works at Red Associates, a strategy consulting company that uses social-science methods (e.g., sense-making and ethnographic research) to give clients an outside view of their business.

78: **Robert J. Sternberg's headhunter story.** Sternberg uses the term *redefining problems,* featuring it as the first of twenty-one research-based strategies he proposes for increasing your creativity. The story is described in Sternberg's *Wisdom, Intelligence, and Creativity Synthesized* (New York: Cambridge University Press, 2003), on page 110 of the 2011 paperback edition. Sternberg's investment theory of creativity is also worth checking out if you are interested in the topic. The theory posits that engaging in innovation is not just an ability but also an individual choice, pointing to the need to consider the—in my eyes very important—cost-benefit aspect of innovating. I wrote more on this in chapter 7 of my first book, *Innovation as Usual: How to Help Your People Bring Great Ideas to Life* (Boston: Harvard Business Review Press, 2013), which I coauthored with Paddy Miller. The insight arguably also applies to reframing and problem solving more generally.

78: **Stephen Hawking's wheelchair.** Intel's unpaid work for Hawking is described by Joao Medeiros in "How Intel Gave Stephen Hawking a Voice," *Wired,* January 2015. Further details are available in the Press section of Intel's website. Many people worked on Hawking's wheelchair. Intel's press releases highlight in particular the work of Intel engineers Pete Denman, Travis Bonifield, Rob Weatherly, and Lama Nachman. Additional details are from my personal conversations with former Intel designer Chris Dame in 2019.

79: **Late-night TV shop commercials.** For more on this, see the "Day 7" chapter of innovation expert Scott Anthony's *The Little Black Book of Innovation: How It Works, How to Do It* (Boston: Harvard Business School Publishing, 2012).

79: **Herminia Ibarra's work.** Ibarra's work on leadership is worth a read: check out her book *Act Like a Leader, Think Like a Leader* (Harvard Business Review Press, 2015).

79: **Martin Seligman on happiness.** See Seligman's book *Flourish: A Visionary New Understanding of Happiness and Well-Being* (New York: Free Press, 2011), or google his "PERMA" framework.

80: **Six factors that lead to professional happiness.** Benjamin Todd and Will MacAskill's research is detailed on their website (80000hours.org). MacAskill's book on effective altruism, *Doing Good Better: How Effective Altruism Can Help You Make a Difference* (New York: Avery, 2015), is also an interesting read and features several examples of reframing (e.g., on how to best use your time and money to do good). Also, "flow" is a well-known concept within the research on happiness: it's when you are doing something so engrossing that you lose yourself in the activity. The term was coined by Mihaly Csikszentmihalyi, who also happens to be one of the key figures within reframing research. Google "flow psychology" for more.

Chapter 6: examine bright spots

84: **Tania and Brian Luna.** Tania Luna shared this story with me in 2018, in a personal conversation and over email. Incidentally, Tania and Brian's story also shows how problem-solving at work and at home are linked. Most

evidently, if you stay up till midnight fighting with your partner at home, odds are you won't perform at your best the next day in the office. More interestingly, the framings and solutions you learn at home can often be used at work too, and vice versa. For example, I spoke to an innovation team who regularly held meetings to decide which projects to stop pursuing. Those meetings were tense and emotionally exhausting, and everyone on the team dreaded them. When did they have them? Late in the afternoon, when everyone's mental surplus was at its lowest.

85: **Chip and Dan Heath.** I borrow the term *bright spots* from Chip and Dan Heath's *Switch: How to Change Things When Change Is Hard* (New York: Broadway Books, 2010), which—along with their book *Decisive: How to Make Better Choices in Life and Work* (New York: Crown Business, 2013)—is highly recommended if you want more advice on problem solving, decision making, and behavior change.

Also, among the strategies I offer here, the bright spots approach is unique in that it won't just help you reframe a problem. Sometimes, it will lead you directly to a viable solution, without any intervening need to reframe (or even understand) the problem—for instance, when the method simply surfaces an existing solution you didn't know about. For anyone but reframing purists, that's of course great news; whatever gets the job done.

85: **Bright spots in medicine.** For an example of this, read the story of Amy Hsia as described in chapter 1 of Lisa Sanders's *Every Patient Tells a Story: Medical Mysteries and the Art of Diagnosis* (New York: Broadway Books, 2009).

85: **Kepner-Tregoe root cause analysis.** Root cause analysis has several founders, but Kepner and Tregoe's *The Rational Manager: A Systematic Approach to Problem Solving and Decision-Making* (New York: McGraw-Hill, 1965) is widely considered the seminal work in the field. The bright spots question (*Where is the problem* not?) is part of their core framework. While Kepner and Tregoe's initial work focused chiefly on problem analysis rather than problem framing, they increasingly addressed reframing in their later work, including *The New Rational Manager* (Princeton, NJ: Princeton Research Press, 1981).

85: **A staple of problem-solving frameworks.** One interesting version of the bright spots strategy is biomimicry: the act of looking for solutions in nature. I have not included this in the main text since biomimicry is arguably of limited use for "everyday" problems, but it has a great track record in the R&D community. One widely known example is the invention of Velcro, inspired by burrs.

Another simple instance of bright spots is of course the idea of "best practices." These can be helpful, and in some industries they have been codified, often by consultants. One interesting version of this is within engineering, where the TRIZ framework, developed by the Soviet engineer Genrikh Altshuller, offers a set of best practices for solving typical engineering problems. The TRIZ method was first described in a paper by Altshuller and R. B. Shapiro, "On the Psychology of Inventive Creation," published in 1956 in the Soviet journal *Voprosi Psichologii*. (*TRIZ*, for the linguistically inclined, is an acronym that stands for "teoriya resheniya izobretatelskikh zadatch," the literal translation of which is "theory of the resolution of invention-related tasks." It is also known as "theory of inventive problem solving.")

86: **Solution-focused brief therapy.** The work of the Milwaukee group is described in Steven de Shazer's books; see *Keys to Solutions in Brief Therapy* (New York: W.W. Norton & Company, 1985) and *Clues: Investigating Solutions in Brief Therapy* (New York: W.W. Norton & Company, 1988). While psychologists today will generally tell you that some issues do indeed require you to explore deeper personality issues, the Milwaukee group's method is now an important and widely recognized tool in the therapist's toolbox. Incidentally, Tania Luna directly credits a member of the Milwaukee group for helping her to become more attuned to bright spots—namely the author and therapist Michele Weiner-Davis, with her advice on "doing more of what's working."

87: **Consider whether you have ever solved a similar problem.** Built upon the work of gestalt psychologist Karl Duncker, a large body of research now exists on the topic of *analogical transfer*, a scientific term for the idea that you can sometimes solve a new problem by asking, *Have I seen problems that are similar to this one?* As with the bright spots strategy in general, it makes a huge difference when you look for those parallels *actively*. They spring to mind much more rarely if you don't seek to make the connections. One famous experiment by Mary L. Gick and Keith J. Holyoak asked people to solve a problem—but before the researchers shared the problem, they asked people to read a few short stories, one of which contained some fairly heavy hints about the solution. As a result, 92 percent of the participants solved the problem—*but only when they were told* that one of the stories they had just read contained a hint. If the researchers did not tell them that, only 20 percent managed to solve the problem. The study is described in two papers: "Analogical Problem Solving," *Cognitive Psychology* 12, no. 3 (1980): 306, and "Schema Induction and Analogical Transfer," *Cognitive Psychology* 15, no. 1 (1983): 1. For an in-depth discussion of Duncker's research and the subsequent work on it, see Richard E. Mayer's *Thinking, Problem Solving, Cognition*, 2nd ed. (New York: Worth Publishers, 1991), pages 50–53 and 415–430.

87: **Greater mental surplus to deal with the stress factors.** Merete Wedell-Wedellsborg, an organizational psychologist and also my amazing sister-in-law, writes about the importance of understanding your "psychological superchargers." These are special (and often idiosyncratic) things that are disproportionately energizing for you. One of Merete's clients, for instance, found it very restorative to browse for potential executive education courses she could sign up for, describing the browsing sessions as a kind of intellectual vacation. See Merete Wedell-Wedellsborg, "How Women at the Top Can Renew Their Mental Energy" (*Harvard Business Review* online, April 16, 2018) for more.

87: **Raquel Rubio Higueras.** The hotel example is from a personal conversation with Raquel Rubio Higueras, 2018.

87: **Long-term thinking in a law firm.** I shared a version of this story in my article "Are You Solving the Right Problems?" *Harvard Business Review*, January–February 2017.

88: **Getting illiterate parents to keep their kids in school.** The Misiones story is recounted in chapter 4 of Richard Pascale, Jerry Sternin, and Monique Sternin's *The Power of Positive Deviance: How Unlikely Innovators Solve the World's Toughest Problems* (Boston: Harvard Business Press, 2010). Based on the authors' deep experience with field work, the book delivers powerful, hands-on advice on how to put the positive deviance approach into practice. The reframing quotation is from page 155 of the 2010 hardcover edition, minor formatting changes have been made for clarity.

89: **50 percent increase in their retention rates.** I have simplified this story somewhat. The full version is very much worth reading, not least for the added detail around how consultants can best work with groups to deploy the positive deviance approach. One central insight (which the authors cover in depth) is the need to let people discover and formulate the insights themselves, rather than having the consultants reframe the problem for them. Also worth noting: while the intervention had demonstrable success and was incredibly cheap (roughly twenty thousand dollars) compared with other projects, the Argentine Ministry of Education didn't support its wider implementation. Why? According to the authors, the government officials were afraid that the method would replace some of the existing million-dollar projects—which the officials grew fat from by siphoning off funds. Perversely, if the method had been a hundred times as expensive as it was, it would have had a better chance of being supported by the officials.

90: **"Conceptual skeleton."** Douglas Hofstadter talks about this in the book he coauthored with Emmanuel Sander, *Surfaces and Essences: Analogy as the Fuel and Fire of Thinking* (New York: Basic Books, 2013). The book delves deeply into the questions of analogy making and categorization, two mental operations that are intricately tied to reframing.

90: **Martin Reeves quotation.** Personal conversation with Martin Reeves, 2019.

91: **pfizerWorks.** The story of pfizerWorks is detailed in a case study written by Paddy Miller and me, "Jordan Cohen at pfizerWorks: Building the Office of the Future," Case DPO-187-E (Barcelona: IESE Publishing, 2009). I edited the quotations for clarity. Some additional details came from my personal conversations with Jordan Cohen, Tanya Carr-Waldron, and Seth Appel, taking place over a period from 2009 to 2018.

91: **Erving Goffman on cultural norms.** Goffman discussed the invisibility of cultural norms in *Behavior in Public Places* (New York: The Free Press, 1963). It has since been studied widely in the sociology literature. See, for instance, the work of Pierre Bourdieu, Harold Garfinkel, and Stanley Milgram.

92: **Broadcast your problem.** The idea of broadcasting problems has been described in a great article by Karim R. Lakhani and Lars Bo Jeppesen, "Getting Unusual Suspects to Solve R&D Puzzles," *Harvard Business Review*, May 2007. Lakhani and Jeppesen studied what happened when companies broadcast their problems on InnoCentive, a popular problem-solving platform: "In a remarkable 30% of cases, problems that could not be solved by experienced corporate research staffs were cracked by nonemployees."

93: **E-850 story.** Part of this story comes from *Innovation as Usual: How to Help Your People Bring Great Ideas to Life* (Boston: Harvard Business Review Press, 2013), which I coauthored with Paddy Miller. The slides themselves were uploaded to Slideshare.com on October 8, 2009, by Erik Pras, the business development manager at DSM who handled the crowdsourcing process. The team did a successful commercial trial in December 2009. They posted the second slide deck (announcing the winners) on February 10, 2010. You can see the full decks by searching for "DSM slideshare Erik Pras" (Pras, 2009). See the next note for the gluey details.

93: **The details of the E-850 reframing.** The E-850 glue, being ecologically friendly, was water-based—and when the laminates were dried after being coated, the water made the wood warp, causing the laminate to fray due to the stresses. Initially, the researchers had framed the problem as, "How do we make the glue stronger so it can withstand the stress of warping?" The solution, however, was found by addressing a different problem—namely preventing the wood from absorbing water, so that the warping didn't happen in the first place (Erik Pras, "DSM NeoResins Adhesive Challenge," October 29, 2009, https://dsmneoresinschallenge.wordpress.com/2009/10/20/hello-world/).

94: **Advice from Dwayne Spradlin.** If you are going to try the tactic of sharing your problem widely, I recommend getting hold of Spradlin's article "Are You Solving the Right Problem?" *Harvard Business Review*, September 2012, in which he shares several helpful pieces of advice on how best to do it. Another useful read is Nelson P. Repenning, Don Kieffer, and Todd Astor's "The Most Underrated Skill in Management," *MIT Sloan Management Review*, Spring 2017.

94: **Negativity bias.** The bias was originally described in the paper "Negativity in Evaluations"; see David E. Kanouse and L. Reid Hanson in *Attribution: Perceiving the Causes of Behaviors*, eds. Edward E. Jones et al. (Morristown, NJ: General Learning Press, 1972). A later paper is also worth reading, as it significantly expands on the concept: Paul Rozin and Edward B. Royzman, "Negativity Bias, Negativity Dominance, and Contagion," *Personality and Social Psychology Review* 5, no. 4 (2001): 296.

Chapter 7: look in the mirror

99: **Fundamental attribution error.** The effect is pervasive. Only when it comes to our *own* bad behaviors do we graciously allow for the possibility that they are the result of special circumstances rather than deep character flaws. The fundamental attribution error was originally documented in a 1967 study by two social psychologists, Edward E. Jones and Victor Harris; see "The Attribution of Attitudes," *Journal of Experimental Social Psychology* 3, no. 1 (1967): 1–24. The actual term was coined later by another social psychologist, Lee Ross; see "The Intuitive Psychologist and His Shortcomings: Distortions in the Attribution Process," in L. Berkowitz, *Advances in Experimental Social Psychology,* vol. 10 (New York: Academic Press, 1977), 173–220.

100: **This pattern continues unabated into adulthood.** Psychologists call the phenomenon "self-serving bias," and it's linked to the fundamental attribution error. For a good overview of the research, see W. Keith Campbell and Constantine Sedikides, "Self-Threat Magnifies the Self-Serving Bias: A Meta-Analytic Integration," *Review of General Psychology* 3, no. 1 (1999): 23–43.

100: **What drivers wrote in their insurance-claim forms.** The quotations are reportedly from a July 26, 1977, article in the *Toronto News* and have been cited in several books, including a psychology textbook. However, I have been unable to track down the original article. Nor could I find evidence of a 1977 newspaper called the *Toronto News*, or for that matter any evidence of a city called Toronto (okay, that last one isn't true). So despite how true-to-life the quotations feel, they are probably anecdotal, which is academic-speak for "complete and utter fiction."

101: **Seek out the pain.** I am normally not one to recommend self-help books. Too often, they are based on shoddy science and magical (meaning rubbish) thinking, and arguably, their advice can at times cause more harm than good. Yet there's one that I found worth reading: *The Tools: Five Tools to Help You Find Courage, Creativity, and Willpower—and Inspire You to Live Life in Forward Motion*, by Phil Stutz and Barry Michels (New York: Spiegel & Grau, 2013). Their first tool, on pain avoidance, explains the concept in a way that I found both memorable and personally useful. Incidentally, their use of simple drawings to illustrate key ideas was an inspiration for the sketches I use in this book.

101: **Have you ever used a dating app?** If the topic of human behavior on dating apps interests you, consider taking a look at Christian Rudder's book *Dataclysm: Love, Sex, Race, and Identity—What Our Online Lives Tell Us about Our Offline Selves* (New York: Crown, 2014). Rudder cofounded the dating site OkCupid and shares a good deal of data—some of it dismal, some of it hilarious—on people's behind-the-scenes dating tactics.

101: **"No drama" people on dating apps.** Meg Joray, a friend and colleague working in public speaking, offered another likely framing: "Maybe these people are expecting their dating experiences to be like a romantic comedy minus the misunderstandings and frictions that always plague a perfect match-up." A great read on this topic is Laura Hilgers's *New York Times* article "The Ridiculous Fantasy of a 'No Drama' Relationship" (July 20, 2019). Hilgers makes a similar point, namely that some people have wildly unrealistic expectations about what real human relationships are like.

102: **Sheila Heen quotation.** Sheila's quotation is from a personal conversation she and I had in 2018. The topic of contribution versus blame is further explored in Douglas Stone, Bruce Patton, and Sheila Heen, *Difficult Conversations: How to Discuss What Matters Most* (New York: Penguin, 1999).

103: **Hans Rosling quotation.** The quotation is from page 207 of *Factfulness: Ten Reasons We're Wrong About the World—and Why Things Are Better Than You Think* (New York: Flatiron Books, 2018), which Hans Rosling coauthored with his son, Ola Rosling, and his daughter-in-law, Anna Rosling Rönnlund. The book is very much worth a read, not just for the insights but also for Hans Rosling's powerful stories from his own life and others'.

103: **"Tell me how the company failed you."** John shared this story with me in a personal conversation in 2018.

103: **"I'll start writing my prize-winning novel . . ."** If you have creative ambitions and the writing example struck a nerve, read Steven Pressfield's *The War of Art: Break Through the Blocks and Win Your Inner Creative Battles* (London:

Orion, 2003). Also read Charles Bukowski's poem "Air and Light and Time and Space," preferably by a lake in Italy.

104: **David Brooks quotation.** The quotation is from his June 7, 2018, column in the *New York Times*, "The Problem With Wokeness."

104: **Wicked problems.** The term *wicked problem* was originally coined by Horst Rittel in 1967, and was described more formally in Horst W. J. Rittel and Melvin M. Webber, "Dilemmas in a General Theory of Planning," *Policy Sciences* 4, no. 2 (1973): 155. On a personal note, I'll admit to feeling ambivalent about the term. Some problems are indeed in a special class, and the paper offers some important insights and distinctions (some of which mirror Jacob Getzels's work on discovered problems). But at the same time, labeling a problem as "wicked" can almost seem like a way to fetishize its complexity, implicitly declaring it unsolvable (much as David Brooks pointed out in the quotation cited above). As students of history will know, we have solved some pretty tough problems over the ages, some of which may well have been considered unsolvable by our predecessors.

104: **Health-care corruption in Ukraine.** See Oliver Bullough, "How Ukraine Is Fighting Corruption One Heart Stent at a Time," *New York Times*, September 3, 2018.

105: **Internal and external self-awareness.** See Tasha Eurich's *Insight: The Surprising Truth About How Others See Us, How We See Ourselves, and Why the Answers Matter More Than We Think* (New York: Currency, 2017).

105: **How to ask for input.** Heidi Grant shared this advice with me in a personal conversation in 2018.

105: **By improving your self-awareness.** For a quick introduction to the topic, including some recommendations of more in-depth exercises, see Adam Grant's "A Better Way to Discover Your Strengths," *Huffpost*, July 2, 2013. A worthwhile deeper dive is Douglas Stone and Sheila Heen's *Thanks for the Feedback: The Science and Art of Receiving Feedback Well* (New York: Viking, 2014). In that book, you'll find tons of helpful advice on how to use (or reject!) feedback you receive from other people.

106: **Having power makes people less capable of understanding others' perspectives.** For the science behind power blindness (my expression, not theirs), see Adam D. Galinsky et al., "Power and Perspectives Not Taken," *Psychological Science* 17, no. 12 (2006): 1068.

Also, at this point, I can't help stealing a Douglas Adams quotation that Heidi Grant shares on page 85 of her book *No One Understands You and What to Do About It* (Boston: Harvard Business Review Press, 2015). The quotation is about horses and goes like this: "They have always understood a great deal more than they let on. It is difficult to be sat on all day, every day, by some other creature, without forming an opinion about them. On the other hand, it is perfectly possible to sit all day, every day, on top of another creature and not have the slightest thought about them whatsoever." Adams originally wrote this in his book *Dirk Gently's Holistic Detective Agency* (New York: Pocket Books, 1987).

106: **Chris Dame story.** The quotations and observations come from a personal conversation with Chris Dame, 2018.

Chapter 8: take their perspective

114: **You can improve your understanding of others.** For an introduction to the research, see Sharon Parker and Carolyn Axtell, "Seeing Another Viewpoint: Antecedents and Outcomes of Employee Perspective Taking," *Academy of Management Journal* 44, no. 6 (2001): 1085.

114: **Increasing your personal exposure.** Studies have found that by engaging in perspective-taking, groups like product-development teams and academic researchers create more-useful output. For an overview, see Adam M. Grant and James W. Berry, "The Necessity of Others Is the Mother of Invention: Intrinsic and Prosocial Motivations, Perspective Taking, and Creativity," *Academy of Management Journal* 54, no. 1 (2011): 73. Beyond providing a helpful summary of the research, Grant and Berry also posit an interesting link between intrinsic motivation, perspective taking, and prosocial motivation, all three of which positively influence the usefulness (and novelty) of the output.

114: **Perspective taking is the cognitive equivalent . . .** Some people discuss perspective taking and empathy as both cognitive processes and behavioral actions—e.g., going out and gaining exposure to people. (A third tradition, not discussed here, looks at empathy as a character trait or disposition.) Given this book's focus on perspective taking as part of a reframing process, I have chosen to use the term to mean the cognitive processes only. Chapter 9, "Move Forward," gets into more action-based ways to discover people's perspectives. The two things are of course related, and the boundary between thinking and doing isn't always as clear-cut as it might seem. Should this stir your interest, check out George Lakoff's work on embodied cognition, *Philosophy in the Flesh*, coauthored with Mark Johnson (New York: Basic Books, 1999), or Andy Clark and David Chalmers's work on the extended mind hypothesis, "The Extended Mind," *Analysis* 58, no. 1, (1998): 7–19.

115: **Nicholas Epley quotation.** The quotation is from N. Epley and E. M. Caruso, "Perspective Taking: Misstepping into Others' Shoes," in K. D. Markman, W. M. P. Klein, and J. A. Suhr, eds., *Handbook of Imagination and Mental Simulation* (New York: Psychology Press, 2009), 295–309. My use of the light-switch metaphor for activating your other-people radar is from the same paper.

115: **"How happy are you?"** See Yechiel Klar and Eilath E. Giladi, "Are Most People Happier Than Their Peers, or Are They Just Happy?" *Personality and Social Psychology Bulletin* 25, no. 5 (1999): 586.

116: **Negative social proof.** See Robert B. Cialdini, *Influence: The Psychology of Persuasion* (New York: Harper Business, 1984). Many other researchers have explored the impact of social proof on adoption. One early example of this is provided by Everett M. Rogers in the classic book *Diffusion of Innovations* (New York: The Free Press, 1962).

116: **Make sure perspective taking happens.** One helpful, more structured framework for doing this is the Jobs-to-

Be-Done method, popularized by innovation experts Clayton Christensen and Michael Raynor in their book *The Innovator's Solution: Creating and Sustaining Successful Growth* (Boston: Harvard Business Press, 2003). Another way to think about it is to draw on Daniel Kahneman's differentiation between System 1 and System 2 thinking. System 1 is fast, effortless, and often inaccurate. System 2 is slow, effortful, and more accurate. Understanding stakeholders is always a task for System 2—the slower, more deliberate approach.

117: **Anchoring and adjustment.** The two-step nature of the process was first pointed out by Daniel Kahneman and Amos Tversky in "Judgment under Uncertainty: Heuristics and Biases," *Science* 185, no. 4157 (1974): 1124.

117: ***"If I were a frontline employee, how would I feel about the reorganization . . ."*** A colleague of mine, Tom Hughes, made the point well in a personal conversation in 2019: "CEOs spend six months pondering whether it makes sense to do a reorganization—and then they launch it, expecting their employees to accept the change after a one-hour all-hands meeting."

118: **People may anchor fairly well, but fail on the adjustment part.** See, for example, Nicholas Epley et al., "Perspective Taking as Egocentric Anchoring and Adjustment," *Journal of Personality and Social Psychology* 87, no. 3 (2004): 327.

119: **Only 2.5 percent of people like to be guinea pigs for new things.** The seminal book on this is Rogers's *Diffusion of Innovations* (mentioned on page 198).

119: **The project team worked *in the same office* as the people they tried—and failed—to recruit.** It's interesting to consider whether familiarity and proximity can sometimes be detrimental to perspective taking. If you live far away from somebody, odds are you'll realize you don't understand that person (triggering an effort to do so). Conversely, if you share an office (or a home) with someone, it's a lot easier to convince yourself that you already understand the person well, hence making you less prone to engage in active perspective taking.

119: **Go beyond your first correct-sounding answer.** Exit interviews are a great example of this. The compensation consultant Jannice Koors, Western Region President of Pearl Meyer, told me, "People tell their companies that they are leaving because they got a better offer—which sounds plausible. But there's almost always more to it than the money. Keep asking." (Personal conversation with Jannice Koors, October 2018.) Nicholas Epley's quote comes from "Perspective Taking as Egocentric Anchoring and Adjustment" (mentioned earlier on this page).

119: **Johannes Hattula's research.** See Johannes D. Hattula et al., "Managerial Empathy Facilitates Egocentric Predictions of Consumer Preferences," *Journal of Marketing Research* 52, no. 2 (2015): 235. The part of the study that found a positive effect of explicitly warning people was conducted with ninety-three marketing managers with a mean age of forty-six years—meaning, they were quite experienced professionals. The exact wording used in the study was, "Recent research has shown that when taking the perspective of consumers, managers frequently fail to suppress their own consumption preferences, needs, and attitudes. Therefore, please do not think about your personal consumption preferences, needs, and attitudes when taking the perspective of the consumer and focus only on the target consumer's preferences, needs, and attitudes."

120: **Jordan Cohen quotes.** Quotes come from my personal conversations with Jordan, 2010.

122: **Rules that are secretly good for you.** This is discussed at length in Richard Thaler and Cass Sunstein's influential book *Nudge: Improving Decisions About Health, Wealth, and Happiness* (New Haven: Yale University Press, 2008). The authors use the term *libertarian paternalism* in cases where the rules suggest a (good) default behavior but leave some leeway for individuals to opt out if they prefer a different option. Other rules, of course, such as speed limits, deliberately don't leave any leeway.

122: **A negative spiral of behavior.** One of the seminal studies of the role of miscommunication in collaborative scenarios was conducted by Robert Axelrod, a key name within game theory and the author of *The Evolution of Cooperation* (New York: Basic Books, 1984). Running simulated collaboration games, like "iterated prisoner's dilemma," Axelrod demonstrated that if there was noise in the model (meaning the potential for misunderstandings), you would perform best by choosing a "forgiving" strategy—that is, by sometimes accepting that mistakes happened, and punishing your opponent only after repeated infractions. Pure "tit for tat" models, in comparison, would often get caught in negative cycles due to an initial misunderstanding.

122: **People's behavior makes sense to them, even if it's problematic overall.** This is one of the essential contributions from what's called public choice theory in political science. Public choice theory arose in the 1950s as researchers started to apply economic principles—including cost-benefit analyses at the individual level—to explain how the state and other institutions made decisions. In particular, it highlighted how individual decision makers sometimes faced incentives that worked against the interests of the broader system.

123: **Rosie Yakob's story.** All quotes are from my personal conversations with Rosie Yakob, 2018.

Chapter 9: move forward

128: **Kevin and Ashley's story.** Personal conversations with Ashley Albert, 2018 and 2019. After crushing her friend Kevin's gelato dreams, Ashley joined him to start a different company that sold matzo. (If you don't know it, matzo is a type of flatbread traditionally consumed during the Jewish holiday Passover.) As Ashley told me, "For ninety years, the market for matzo had been dominated by two players, and in my opinion, there was room for creating a more appetizing kind of matzo." To move forward, Ashley and Kevin created a simple test of their idea: they cooked up a batch of matzo crackers, created appealing, off-beat packaging for them, and

then tried selling them to four local store owners. The matzo boxes sold out quickly, making the owners ask, "Can you sell me four crates next week?" A fancy artisanal food show and press mentions followed. A year later, the matzo boxes had been featured twice on Oprah Winfrey's list "Oprah's Favorite Things," and as of this writing, the product is sold in more than eight hundred stores across the United States, and can also be found in the UK, Canada, Spain and Japan. If it hadn't been for Ashley's insistence on validating the problem, Kevin might be scraping by instead selling coffee in an empty gelato store.

129: **Chris Voss and labeling in hostage situations.** The method is described in chapter 3 of Voss's book *Never Split the Difference: Negotiating as if Your Life Depended on It* (New York: HarperCollins, 2016).

130: **Steve Blank and problem meetings.** The method is described in chapter 5 of Steve Blank and Bob Dorf's book *The Startup Owner's Manual: The Step-By-Step Guide for Building a Great Company* (Pescadero, CA: K&S Ranch Publishing, 2012). Grab hold of this book if you are building a startup.

130: **Cisco case.** The Cisco case is based on Paddy Miller and Thomas Wedell-Wedellsborg, "Start-up Cisco: Deploying Start-up Methods in a Giant Company," Case DPO-426-E (Barcelona: IESE Publishing, May 2018); minor formatting changes have been made for clarity. Additional quotes by Oseas are from my personal conversation with Oseas Ramírez Assad, 2019.

131: **Georgina de Rocquigny story.** Personal conversation with Georgina de Rocquigny, 2017.

133: **Saman Rahmanian and Dan Teran.** I know Saman and Dan from Prehype, the company where they met and to which I serve as an adviser. I was not personally involved in the Managed by Q story, but I have followed their journey since they launched in their first office. The quotations are from an unpublished case I wrote after interviewing Saman in January 2016. Parts of the story have also been featured in several books, including Zeynep Ton's *The Good Jobs Strategy: How the Smartest Companies Invest in Employees* *to Lower Costs and Boost Profits* (Boston: New Harvest, 2014).

134: **Reported to be over $200 million.** The sales figure has not been made public, but according to the financial data company Pitchbook, Managed by Q was valued at $249 million a few months prior to the acquisition. See https://pitchbook.com/profiles/company/65860-66.

134: **A method called pretotyping.** For more on pretotyping, see Alberto Savoia's book *The Right It: Why So Many Ideas Fail and How to Make Sure Yours Succeed* (New York: HarperOne, 2019).

135: **Wine stopper story.** Personal conversation with Henrik Werdelin, 2019. The team consisted of Matt Meeker, Carly Strife, Mikkel Holm Jensen, Suzanne McDonnell, Christina Donnelly, Becky Segal, Michael Novotny, Jeffrey Awong, Melissa Seligmann, and John Toth.

135: **Scott McGuire's story.** Personal conversation with Scott McGuire, November 2018.

136: **Freezing the problem.** The Kees Dorst quotation is from chapter 1 of his book *Frame Innovation: Create New Thinking by Design* (Cambridge, MA: Massachusetts Institute of Technology, 2015).

Chapter 10: three tactical challenges

145: **Multiplying problems.** After a discussion on reframing, a Prehype partner by the name of Tom Le Bree sent me the following note: "If you are still looking for book titles, I'd like to put forward *I've Got 99 Problems, but I Only Started with 1*."

146: **Occam's razor.** Yes, people spell it "Occam's razor" even though the friar's name was William of Ockham. I say Ockham got off lightly. With a surname like Wedell-Wedellsborg, if I'm remembered at all, odds are it'll be as "err, the reframing guy."

146: **Steve de Shazer quotation.** The quotation is from page 16 of de Shazer's book *Keys to Solution in Brief Therapy* (New York: W. W. Norton & Company, 1985). Despite the formulation of the quotation, de Shazer doesn't suggest that this is *always* true, merely that it's often true. It is part of his bigger point about how traditional psychologists too often believe that "complex" problems should have equally complex solutions, rather than first testing out simpler approaches.

147: **Bolsa Familia program.** The program has been widely described by now. A simple Google search will give you the basics. If you want more detail, I recommend reading chapter 1 of Jonathan Tepperman's *The Fix: How Countries Use Crises to Solve the World's Worst Problems* (New York: Tim Duggan Books, 2016). The studies and data I mention are taken from pages 39–41 of Tepperman's book.

149: **Sir Kensington's story.** Personal conversations with Mark Ramadan and Scott Norton, 2014.

150: **Creating growth via ethnographic methods.** For a good exploration of how deep-dive ethnographic methods can reveal new sources of growth, I recommend *The Moment of Clarity: Using the Human Sciences to Solve Your Toughest Business Problems*, by Christian Madsbjerg and Mikkel B. Rasmussen (Boston: Harvard Business Review Press, 2014). The authors also share some interesting examples on how to work with framing. One is the example of LEGO, the toymaker, in which they reframed the research question from "What toys do kids want?" to "What is the role of play?" (See chapter 5 of their book.) If you are a senior executive, another worthwhile read is *Discovery-Driven Growth: A Breakthrough Process to Reduce Risk and Seize Opportunity* (Boston: Harvard Business Review Press, 2009), by Rita Gunther McGrath and Ian C. MacMillan, in which the authors share a good deal of helpful advice on how to structure organizations for discovery.

151: **Edgar Schein and humble inquiry.** Schein's book *Humble Inquiry: The Gentle Art of Asking Instead of Telling* (San Francisco: Berrett-Koehler Publishers, 2013) provides one good and fairly short introduction to the art of asking better questions. Other recent contributors include Warren Berger and Hal Gregersen.

151: **Amy Edmondson and psychological safety.** See Amy Edmondson's book *The Fearless Organization* (Hoboken, NJ: Wiley, 2019), or google the term "psychological safety" for a quick introduction.

151: **Hal Gregersen and seeking out discomfort.** The research is summarized in Gregersen's article "Bursting the CEO Bubble," *Harvard Business Review*, March–April 2017.

151: **Jeremiah Zinn's story.** I have shared parts of Jeremiah's story in my article "Are You Solving the Right Problems?" *Harvard Business Review*, January–February 2017.

154: **"Teams that are diverse outperform teams whose members are more similar to each other."** There is a large body of research on the role of diversity and inclusion in problem solving. If you wish to delve deeper into this research, I recommend Scott Page's book *The Diversity Bonus: How Great Teams Pay Off in the Knowledge Economy* (Princeton, NJ: Princeton University Press, 2017), which provides a good, nuanced overview of the topic, including things like what diversity actually is (e.g., social diversity versus cognitive diversity), what types of problems diversity is most helpful with (nonroutine knowledge work), and much else. I owe thanks to Susanne Justesen of Copenhagen Business School for pointing me to Scott Page's work.

154: **Marc Granger story.** The story comes from a client engagement I did when I first started doing research into innovation. Part of the case is described in my first book, *Innovation as Usual: How to Help Your People Bring Great Ideas to Life*, as well as in my article "Are You Solving the Right Problems?" *Harvard Business Review*, January–February 2017.

156: **Getting ideas from extreme outsiders.** One early example took place in 1714 when the British Parliament requested help in figuring out how ships could determine their longitude at sea. The solution came from a Yorkshire clockmaker, John Harrison. For more on the power of extreme outsiders, read Karim Lakhani and Lars Bo Jeppesen's article "Getting Unusual Suspects to Solve R&D Puzzles," *Harvard Business Review*, May 2007.

156: **Boundary spanners.** Michael Tushman coined the term in a paper from 1977; see Michael L. Tushman, "Special Boundary Roles in the Innovation Process," *Administrative Science Quarterly* 22, no. 4 (1977): 587–605. The underlying idea of boundary spanners has been around since the early days of research into innovation.

157: **Restating your problem in less specialized terms.** For a useful discussion of this, including an example, see Dwayne Spradlin's article "Are You Solving the Right Problem?" *Harvard Business Review*, September 2012.

Chapter 11: when people resist reframing

162: **If you are lucky, trust exists between you and the owner of the problem.** One useful theoretical model distinguishes among three types of trust: trust in **honesty** (*If I forgot my wallet, would you return it?*), trust in **competence** (*Are you capable of getting the job done?*), and people's trust in your **intentions toward them** (*If something goes wrong, will you have my back?*). Even world-class experts with a record of perfect integrity may be distrusted if people suspect the experts don't really care about them. See Roger C. Mayer, James H. Davis, and F. David Schoorman, "An Integrative Model of Organizational Trust," *Academy of Management Review* 20, no. 3 (1995): 709–734, for the three-part model above, or Rachel Botsman's *Who Can You Trust?: How Technology Brought Us Together and Why It Might Drive Us Apart* (New York: PublicAffairs, 2017) for a more recent, broad-audience discussion.

164: **Clay Christensen and Andy Grove.** Clayton Christensen shared this story at an event I attended in London on September 10, 2013.

164: **Promotion/prevention.** For more on promotion/prevention focus, read Heidi Grant and E. Tory Higgins's "Do You Play to Win—or to Not Lose?" *Harvard Business Review*, March 2013, or read Higgins's "Promotion and Prevention:

Regulatory Focus as a Motivational Principle," *Advances in Experimental Social Psychology* 30 (1998): 1.

164: **Closure avoidance.** The concept was originally developed by Arie W. Kruglanski, Donna M. Webster, and Adena Klem in "Motivated Resistance and Openness to Persuasion in the Presence or Absence of Prior Information," *Journal of Personality and Social Psychology* 65, no. 5 (1993): 861, and has since been elaborated on by other researchers.

165: **Tolerance for frustration and ambiguity.** For an example of the research into ambiguity and its connection to creative problem solving, see Michael D. Mumford et al., "Personality Variables and Problem-Construction Activities: An Exploratory Investigation," *Creativity Research Journal* 6, no. 4 (1993): 365. The management thinker Roger L. Martin has also explored this in depth, sharing how expert problem solvers work with ambiguity in practice. See his book *The Opposable Mind: How Successful Leaders Win Through Integrative Thinking* (Boston: Harvard Business Review Press, 2009).

166: **Many nineteenth-century doctors were reluctant to recognize . . .** One poignant example is provided by Charles Delucena Meigs, an august physician who, in 1854, confidently rejected the emerging germ theory of disease with the immortal—and also literally mortal—words, "Doctors are gentlemen, and gentlemen's hands are clean"; see C. D. Meigs, *On the Nature, Signs, and Treatment of Childbed Fevers* (Philadelphia: Blanchard and Lea, 1854), 104. I wrote about the slow adoption of medical handwashing in chapter 5 of *Innovation as Usual*. For a brief introduction, google "Ignaz Semmelweis," a physician whose tragic story offers lessons about innovation in the medical world.

166: **Upton Sinclair quotation.** The quotation is from Sinclair's *I, Candidate for Governor: And How I Got Licked*, published by the author in 1934 and republished in 1994 by the University of California Press. The quotation is on page 109 of the 1994 version.

166: **The allure of certainty.** For the science behind this, see Robert A. Burton's *On Being Certain: Believing You Are Right Even When You're Not* (New York: St. Martin's Press, 2008).

167: **Floppy-disk anecdote.** Personal conversation with Chris Dame, 2019, at The Royal Palms Shuffleboard Club.

168: **CIA story.** The story is recounted on pages 109–113 of de Shazer's book *Clues: Investigating Solutions in Brief Therapy* (New York: W. W. Norton & Company, 1988).

169: **Anthony's story.** Personal conversation with the cofounder, October 2018.

170: **Samsung story.** Personal conversation with Luke Mansfield, 2013. The full story is described in Paddy Miller and Thomas Wedell-Wedellsborg, "Samsung's European Innovation Team," Case DPO-0307-E (Barcelona: IESE Publishing, 2014).

Conclusion: a word in parting

174: **Thomas Chamberlin.** The quotations, as well as the information I share, are from Chamberlin's "The Method of Multiple Working Hypotheses," *Science* 15 (1890): 92. The paper is still eminently readable and offers a fascinating window into the mind of a contemporary of Charles Darwin, Marie Curie, and William James. You can find it by searching for his name and the title of the paper. I owe thanks to Roger Martin's *The Opposable Mind: How Successful Leaders Win Through Integrative Thinking* (Boston: Harvard Business Review Press, 2009) for bringing Chamberlin's work to my attention.

174: **The dangers of a single working hypothesis.** For a wonderful example—an example that may have inspired Chamberlin's thinking—read Louis Menand's book *The Metaphysical Club: A Story of Ideas in America* (New York: Farrar, Straus and Giroux, 2001), paying special attention to the character of Louis Agassiz. Agassiz was a gifted and charismatic natural scientist with a "deliciously imperfect" command of English and some completely wrongheaded ideas about science. Faced with mounting evidence that his grand theory was wrong, Agassiz firmly rejected all alternative theories (including one offered by a certain Charles Darwin) and instead organized a months-long trip to Brazil to search for confirming evidence of his own theory. He didn't find it, and while he was out of town, pretty much everyone quickly agreed that Darwin was right and Agassiz wrong. (His story is told from page 97 onward in the 2002 paperback edition.)

175: **Chamberlin's list.** Building on Chamberlin's comparison to love, I can't help remarking that if you replace *explanation* with *partner*, the bulleted list can also double as a fairly apt description of certain contemporary dating practices.

index

acknowledgments

Without Paddy Miller, incomparable as he was, this book would never have come to be. Paddy started out as my teacher and eventually became my colleague, coauthor, mentor, and friend. As I was finishing this book, Paddy passed away from heart failure at age 71. Warm, funny, brilliant, creative, deeply caring, and a little bit bonkers in the best possible way, Paddy is sorely missed by Sara, George, Seb, me, and the many other people whose lives he touched and made better. This book is dedicated to him.

Many other people helped shape the ideas in this book. **Douglas Stone** and **Sheila Heen**, of the Harvard Negotiation Project, provided incisive, game-changing guidance on everything from titling to thinky-thoughts thinking (Sheila, as it happens, is the one I have to thank for suggesting the book's title.) **Melinda Merino** at Harvard Business Review Press saw the potential in reframing early on, and she and HBR editors **David Champion** and **Sarah Green Carmichael** helped shape the initial incarnations of my work. My stellar book editor, **Scott Berinato**, patiently shepherded me through the publishing process, made the book much better, and gently told me no when I wanted to add forty pages of research appendixes, 3-D images, and secret lemon-juice writing. **Jennifer Waring** kept a very complicated production process expertly and miraculously on track, leaving no detail unattended.

Esmond Harmsworth, of Aevitas Creative Management, remains the best possible agent an author could wish for. Prehype's **Henrik Werdelin** continues to be a key thinking partner on reframing and much else. He is finally publishing his own book, *The Acorn Method*, and it deserves to be very widely read while still selling slightly fewer copies than mine.

The book also benefited immensely from a dedicated group of people who volunteered to provide detailed feedback on the manuscript: **Fritz Gugelmann**, **Christian Budtz**, **Anna Ebbesen**, **Marija Silk**, **Mette Walter Werdelin**, **Simon Schultz**, **Philip Petersen**, **Meg Joray**, **Roger Hallowell**, **Dana Griffin**, **Oseas Ramírez Assad**, **Rebecca Lea Myers**, **Casper Willer**, **Concetta Morabito**, **Damon Horowitz**, **Heidi Grant**, and **Emily Holland Hull**. A special thanks goes to **Scott Anthony**, of Innosight, whose expert feedback also helped sharpen the ideas of my first book.

For taking a chance on my hand-drawn project and for bringing it to life in such a beautiful way, I also owe thanks to the wider team at **Harvard Business Review**

Group and beyond: Stephani Finks, Jon Zobenica, Allison Peter, Alicyn Zall, Julie Devoll, Erika Heilman, Sally Ashworth, Jon Shipley, Alexandra Kephart, Brian Galvin, Felicia Sinusas, Ella Morrish, Akila Balasubramaniyan, Lindsey Dietrich, Ed Domina, and Ralph Fowler.

My thinking on reframing has also been shaped by people at four other organizations. At **Duke Corporate Education**, I owe thanks to both current and former collaborators: Julie Okada, Shannon Knott, Pete Gerend, Ed Barrows, Nancy Keeshan, Dawn Shaw, Nikki Bass, Erin Bland Baker, Mary Kay Leigh, Heather Leigh, Emmy Melville, Melissa Pitzen, Tarry Payton, Jane Sommers-Kelly, Jane Boswick-Caffrey, Tiffany Burnette, Richelle Hobbs Lidher, Holly Anastasio, Karen Royal, Joy Monet Saunders, Christine Robers, Kim Taylor-Thompson, and Michael Chavez. At **IESE Business School**: Tricia Kullis, Mike Rosenberg, Kip Meyer, John Almandoz, Stefania Randazzo, Jill Limongi, Elisabeth Boada, Josep Valor, Eric Weber, Julie Cook, Giuseppe Auricchio, Mireia Rius, Aniya Iskhakava, Alejandro Lago, Sebastien Brion, Roser Marimón-Clos Sunyol, Núria Taulats, Noelia Romero Galindo, Gemma Colobardes, Maria Gábarron, and Christine Ecker. At **BarkBox**: Stacie Grissom, Suzanna Schumacher, and Mikkel Holm Jensen. At **Prehype**: Stacey Seltzer, Saman Rahmanian, Dan Teran, Amit Lubling, Stuart Willson, Zachariah Reitano, Richard Wilding, and Nicholas Thorne.

An even larger group of people have been part of the reframing journey in ways big and small: Tom Kalil, Richard Straub, Ilse Straub, Linda Vidal, Jordan Cohen, Christian Madsbjerg, Mikkel B. Rasmussen, Julian Birkinshaw, Dorie Clark, Bob Sutton, Ori Brafman, Christoffer Lorenzen, Maria Fiorini, Cecilie Muus Willer, Anders Ørjan Jensen, Marie Kastrup, Julie Paulli Budtz, Christian Ørsted, Edward Elson, Martin Roll, Blathnaid Conroy, Nicole Abi-Esber, Christiane Vejlø, Tania Luna, Ashley Albert (and Elliott), Ea Ryberg Due, Claus Mossbeck, Joy Caroline Morgan, Sophie Jourlait-Filéni, Julia June Bossman, Lydia Laurenson, Lise Lauridsen, Pilar Marquez, Carlos Alban, Laurent van Lerberghe, Esteban Plata, Alberto Colzi, Ryan Quigley, Brendan McAtamney, Beatriz Loeches, Jack Coyne, Chris Dame, Ulrik Trolle, Peter Heering, Susanne Justesen, Julie Wedell-Wedellsborg, Morten Meisner, Kristian Hart-Hansen, Silvia Bellezza, Elizabeth Webb, Astrid Sandoval, Paul Jeremaes, Ali Gelles, Joy Holloway, Linda Lader, Phil Lader, Stephen Kosslyn, Robin S. Rosenberg, Kelly Glynn, Kevin Engholm, Megan Spath, Per von Zelowitz, David Dabscheck, Judy Durkin, Tracey Madden, Jennifer Squeglia, Heidi Germano, Kathrin Hassemer, Lynden Tennison, Lynn Kelley, Dave Bruno, Teresa Marshall, Karen Strating, Tom Hughes, Jared Bleak, Bruce McBratney, Roz Savage, Lilac Nachum, Linni Rita Gad, Jens Hillingsø, Martin Nordestgaard Knudsen, Luke Mansfield, Jerome Wouters, Ran Merkazy, Erich Joachimsthaler, Agathe Blanchon-Ehrsam, Olivia Haynie, Kenneth Mikkelsen, Brian Palmer, Michelle Blieberg, Josefin Holmberg, Kate Dee, Amy Brooks, Nikolai Brun, Justin Finkelstein, Jennifer Falkenberg, Thomas Gillet, Barbara Scheel Agersnap, Nicolas Boalth, Hanne Merete Lassen, Jens Kristian

Jørgensen, Axel Rosenø, Sarah Bay-Andersen, Colin Norwood, Joan Kuhl, Kellen D. Sick, Svetlana Bilenkina, Braden Kelley, Chuck Appleby, Thomas Jensen, Shelie Gustafson, Heather Wishart-Smith, Michael Hathorne, Jona Wells, Paul Thies, Eric Wilhelm, Christy Canida, Raman Frey, Olivia Nicol, Mie Olise Kjærgaard, Maggie Dobbins, Phil Matsheza, Dawn Del Rio, Patricia Perlman, Nils Rørbæk Petersen, Claus Albrektsen, Lisbet Borker, Kim Vejen, Niels Jørgen Engel, and Birgit Løndahl. Rucola's team kept me fed: Amy Richardson, Jon Calhoun, Bryan Sloss, Allie Huggins, Jeremiah Gorbold, Fernando Sanchez, Jarett Gibson, Brian Bennett, Greg Lauro, and Shevawn Norton. The amazing photographer Gregers Heering is responsible for the author photo. Mikael Olufsen, of course, continues to be the world's best godfather.

Finally, it's said that we don't choose our families. But if we could, I'd still chose the one I have because they are really, really fantastic: my parents Gitte and Henrik, my brother Gregers, my sister-in-law Merete, and the whole extended WW-and-beyond family mafia. And to my nephew and nieces, Clara, Carl-Johan, and Arendse: I love you and I'm very much looking forward to seeing what you'll get up to. I feel lucky to have all of you in my life.

about the author

Thomas Wedell-Wedellsborg has spent the last decade studying the practical aspects of innovation and problem solving in the workplace. His research has been featured in *Harvard Business Review*, the *Sunday Times*, the *Telegraph*, the BBC, *Bloomberg Businessweek*, and the *Financial Times*. With Paddy Miller, he co-authored *Innovation as Usual* (Harvard Business Review Press, 2013) on the art of leading innovation.

As a speaker and executive adviser, Wedell-Wedellsborg has shared and refined his reframing method with clients all over the world, including Cisco, Microsoft, Citigroup, Time Warner, AbbVie, Caterpillar, Amgen, Prudential, Union Pacific, Credit Suisse, Deloitte, the *Wall Street Journal*, and the United Nations.

Prior to his current career, Wedell-Wedellsborg served as an officer with the Danish Royal Guards. He holds an MBA from IESE Business School and an MA from the University of Copenhagen. Originally from Denmark, he lives in New York and travels globally for speaking engagements.

For more information and speaking requests, visit www.thomaswedell.com.

Frame

What's the problem?

Who is involved?

Reframe

Look outside the frame

Rethink the goal → ?

Examine bright spots ✗ ✗ ✓ ✗

Look in the mirror

Take their perspective

Move forward

How do we keep momentum?

Frame

What's the problem?

Who is involved?

Reframe

Look outside the frame

Rethink the goal

Examine bright spots ✗ ✗ ✓ ✗

Look in the mirror

Take their perspective

Move forward

How do we keep momentum?

Frame

What's the problem?

Who is involved?

Reframe

Look outside the frame

Rethink the goal

Examine bright spots

Look in the mirror

Take their perspective

Move forward

How do we keep momentum?

Frame

What's the problem?

Who is involved?

Reframe

Look outside the frame

Rethink the goal ⟶ ?

Examine bright spots ✗ ✗ ✓ ✗

Look in the mirror

Take their perspective

Move forward

How do we keep momentum?

Frame

What's the problem?

Who is involved?

?

Reframe

Look outside the frame

Rethink the goal

Examine bright spots ✗ ✗ ✓ ✗

Look in the mirror

Take their perspective

Move forward

How do we keep momentum?

⇨

Frame

What's the problem?

Who is involved?

Reframe

Look outside the frame

Rethink the goal ⟶ ?

Examine bright spots ✗ ✗ ✓ ✗

Look in the mirror

Take their perspective

Move forward

How do we keep momentum?

Reframing checklist

Frame the problem
What's the problem? Who's involved?

Look outside the frame
What are we missing?

Rethink the goal
Is there a better goal to pursue?

Examine bright spots
Are there positive exceptions?

Look in the mirror
What is my role in creating the problem?

Take their perspective
What problem are they trying to solve?

Move forward
How do we keep momentum?

Reframing checklist

Frame the problem
What's the problem? Who's involved?

Look outside the frame
What are we missing?

Rethink the goal
Is there a better goal to pursue?

Examine bright spots
Are there positive exceptions?

Look in the mirror
What is my role in creating the problem?

Take their perspective
What problem are they trying to solve?

Move forward
How do we keep momentum?